ENDORSEMENTS

I have known Mark for decades, and he has always had a passion to help the people and organizations he has worked with to fulfill their God-given potential. Through *The Coach Approach*, Mark gives amazing insights and practical wisdom in how we can each coach or influence others, and thus, the teams we/they lead to be all God created them to be.

Frank Kelly III
CEO, Kelly Benefits

Coach Mark Stephens has put together a brilliantly simple, action-oriented, practical read on coaching for leaders. If you lead, manage, or influence others, and want to integrate coaching into your leadership toolkit, this is the book for you. Utilizing his talent for storytelling, Mark inspires with real life examples that all of us can implement. *The Coach Approach* is your guidebook to becoming a leader who increases productivity and effectiveness, while also growing and empowering people.

Tina Stoltzfus Horst, M.S.
Author of Dancing between Cultures: Culturally Intelligent
Coaching for Missions and Ministry;
Founder, Coaching Mission International

A **better way** to lead
in business and beyond

The
COACH
APPROACH

Coach M

MARK STEPHENS

Published by Two Penny Publishing
850 E Lime Street #266
Tarpon Springs, FL 34688
TwoPennyPublishing.com
info@twopennypublishing.com

For permission requests and ordering information, email the publisher at:
info@twopennypublishing.com

Headshot Photo by Empire Photography
"The COACH Model" graphic by K. E. Webb
"Heart Romantic Love" graphic by Vecteezy.com
"Psychology and business head icon set" graphic by Vecteezy.com

Scripture quotations marked (CSB) have been taken from the Christian Standard Bible®, Copyright © 2017 by Holman Bible Publishers. Used by permission. Christian Standard Bible® and CSB® are federally registered trademarks of Holman Bible Publishers.

Scripture quotations marked (ESV) are from The ESV® Bible (The Holy Bible, English Standard Version®), copyright © 2001 by Crossway, a publishing ministry of Good News Publishers. Used by permission. All rights reserved.

Scripture quotations marked (KJV) are taken from The Authorized (King James) Version. Rights in the Authorized Version in the United Kingdom are vested in the Crown. Reproduced by permission of the Crown's patentee, Cambridge University Press

Scripture quotations marked (NIV) are taken from the Holy Bible, New International Version®, NIV®. Copyright © 1973, 1978, 1984, 2011 by Biblica, Inc.™ Used by permission of Zondervan. All rights reserved worldwide. www.zondervan.com The "NIV" and "New International Version" are trademarks registered in the United States Patent and Trademark Office by Biblica, Inc.™

Scripture quotations marked (NLT) are taken from the Holy Bible, New Living Translation, copyright ©1996, 2004, 2015 by Tyndale House Foundation. Used by permission of Tyndale House Publishers, Carol Stream, Illinois 60188. All rights reserved.

ISBN: 978-1-950995-79-0
eBook also available

Library of Congress Control Number: 2022915525

FIRST EDITION

For more information about the author or to book him for your next event or media interview, please contact his representative at: info@twopennypublishing.com

Two Penny Publishing is a partnership publisher of a variety of genres. We help first-time and seasoned authors share their stories, passion, knowledge, and experiences that help others grow and learn. Please visit our website: TwoPennyPublishing.com if you would like us to consider your manuscript or book idea for publishing.

My book is dedicated to Dad and Mom. Nearly thirty years ago, Dad, you planted the seed of writing a book in me. Words are powerful. I have never forgotten that moment of encouragement and belief in me, and I am forever grateful for your steadfast love and support. I love you, Mom and Dad.

TABLE OF CONTENTS

Foreword 9

Introduction 13

PART ONE: POSSIBILITIES 21

Chapter 1: Growth Mindset vs. Fixed Mindset. 25
Chapter 2: Believe Something Different is Possible 33
Chapter 3: Act Differently. 41

PART TWO: POSTURE 53

HEAD
Chapter 4: Curious 57
Chapter 5: Active Listening 65
Chapter 6: Think Differently. 77

HEART
Chapter 7: Humble / Wanting the Best for Others. 87
Chapter 8: Empathy / Selflessness. 97
Chapter 9: Self Control / Patience 107

PART THREE: PROCESS 117

    Chapter 10: Outcome 121

    Chapter 11: Awareness 129

    Chapter 12: Action Steps 137

PART FOUR: PIVOT........................... 147

    Chapter 13: Application 151

    Chapter 14: Habits 163

    Chapter 15: Mistakes People Make............... 173

    Chapter 16: Pro Tools and Tips.................. 179

End Notes...................................... 185

Acknowledgments................................ 189

About the Author 191

FOREWORD

On average, you and I will have 30 conversations and say about 16,000 words today. In a year, these words would fill 132 books with 400 pages each. We spend roughly 20 percent of our lives yakking away. We love talking, telling, and impressing others with how much we know. This is life.

For most of us, we do this because we truly believe our words help and add value. However, have you considered that you may be hurting and not helping? Maybe showing up and zipping the lip, listening with attentive ears and an open heart, is a better way to show you care. God gave us two ears and one mouth for a reason – perhaps He wants us to listen twice as much as talk.

In James 1:19 (CSB), words from the brother of Jesus challenge us: "My dear brothers and sisters, understand this: Everyone should be quick to listen, slow to speak, and slow to anger." This is incredible wisdom for those of us who love to blab all the time. It is the Quick-Slow-Slow strategy. Quick to listen, slow to speak, and slow to become angry. Unfortunately, I usually do the Slow-Quick-Quick strategy: Slow to listen, quick to speak, and yes, quick to get angry.

For more than 30 years, I have led thousands of leaders in over 100 countries, and I know that James' wisdom works. When leaders are quick to listen, slow to speak, and slow to anger, God uses them in powerful ways and leaders grow. Instead of talking and telling people what to do (The Tell Approach), leaders who listen and ask (The Coach Approach) see more transformation. The Coach Approach is definitely harder, but it's way more impactful and rewarding.

I first heard and learned about the Coach Approach from my friend, Mark Stephens, whom I've ministered alongside for 32 years. Even though he isn't the creator of leadership coaching, he has developed this simple but powerful leadership style that can change you and the people you lead. Ten years ago, he began his own journey to discover the power of leadership coaching, and he shared it with me. The Coach Approach is transformational because it embraces:

More curiosity.
More listening.
More questions.
More humility.
More empathy.
More self-control.

As a leader, I've watched Mark move from being a classic Tell Approach leader to a Coach Approach leader. As we have taken many trips throughout Asia together over the last 10 years, I have seen his leadership change first-hand. Many times, I wanted to interject myself and give the answers. But Mark is patient, he listens intently, and he asks questions. His process usually takes longer, but it's a better way. Those he leads walk away changed, stronger than they would have been had he told them the answers. I have witnessed the power of the Coach Approach, and I am now committed to becoming a Coach Approach leader too.

The book you are holding is packed with powerful principles, insights, and stories to help you become a transformational leader. You will be challenged and encouraged as Mark shares with authenticity and transparency about his own leadership experiences. *The Coach Approach* provides quick and insightful tools you can immediately implement into your day-to-day life. It is a book you will want to keep nearby so you can reference it often on your leadership journey.

It's time to zip the lip and start listening with attentive ears! *The Coach Approach* will change you, your teams, your co-workers, and your family. Guaranteed. Let's go! We can do this.

Enjoy the journey,

DAN BRITTON

Chief Field Officer of Fellowship of Christian Athletes and author of seven books including bestseller *One Word That Will Change Your Life*.

INTRODUCTION

I was ready for a change. After reading the book *Living Forward* by Michael Hyatt and Daniel Harkavy, I listened to a podcast about executing your life plan. During the show, the hosts mentioned a 1-800 number to call if you wanted help with putting together and achieving your life plan. I called the number, and they offered to pair me with a life coach. I loved the book, and creating and executing a life plan resonated with me; so, I jumped in with both feet. I hired a coach and never looked back. It was one of the most impactful decisions I have ever made.

At that time, I was in a season of reflecting on my life and trying to determine the legacy I wanted to leave to God, my wife, my parents, my girls, my co-workers, and my friends. My coach walked with me and challenged me during our times together, helping me develop a life plan. This plan helped me start with the end of my life and work backwards, assembling an action plan about the legacy I hope to leave. It was an amazing process that I believe would benefit everyone.

During my coaching sessions, we often talked about my work with the Fellowship of Christian Athletes (FCA), focusing on my role of serving international leaders. Six months into our coaching sessions, my coach, Dick Savidge, suggested I become a coach because it could help me lead my Southeast Asia leaders.

He said, "You should be a coach. You are not really managing them from this far and you aren't really leading them. The best way to get the most out of your leaders in Southeast Asia is to lead with The Coach Approach." As FCA's Mid-Atlantic Director of International Advancement, I work closely with each country's National Directors, the highest level leaders within their respective countries who are developing other leaders. Older and more experienced than many of the National Directors, it was tempting to take an approach to leadership that I'd experienced for much of my life: tell them what to do and how to do it. But, because of our different cultures and contexts, utilizing my own ideas and experiences was not the best way to approach their work. Taking the Coach Approach—being curious, employing active listening, and asking powerful questions— became a better way to serve them.

Becoming a life coach turned me into an avid learner. I read more than ten books on coaching and other various articles. I also listened to countless podcasts and engaged in training from Keith Webb and Charles Hooper Jr. at Creative Results Management. Coaching became my passion, so much so that I became a certified coach by the largest governing body of coaches: the International Coaching Federation (ICF).

I have been coaching for many years now, utilizing the skills I learned through ICF certified training. I have often found myself in a coaching session encouraging those I am coaching to take the Coach Approach in leading his or her team. Facing these situations again and again, I decided to write *The Coach Approach* to help all leaders become stronger and more effective.

If you lead in any capacity—as a CEO, school principal, manager, sports coach, pastor, supervisor, influencer—this book is for you. The Coach Approach centers around four key concepts that will assist and accelerate your leadership.

First, I will share the **Possibilities** that abound as you lead in this new way. Second, I explore the **Posture** needed to make sure your head and heart are in the right spot. Third, you will learn a basic **Process** for coaching others. Fourth, I will help you **Pivot** to coaching. Finally, I will show you some tools you will need to implement The Coach Approach.

My hope is that you will experience the same kind of life transformation I did when I got into coaching, and that you'll share this approach with others. It will challenge them, help them grow, and help their teams. I once heard a CFO ask a CEO, "What happens if we invest in developing our people and they leave us?" The CEO replied, "What happens if we don't, and they stay?" You must invest in your team. Investing in your people equals investing in your organization.

You may be reading this book because you want to make improvements personally or within your organization. I commend you for that. This reminds me of a quote I often heard from Coach Les Steckel, the former president of FCA and a football coach for 45 years, including 7 NFL teams: "We all want progress. It is change we don't like." This may make you laugh like it makes me laugh. Of course, I want progress. Of course, I want to improve and get better. Yet, I can also be resistant to change. **Change will be the key to progress and leading your**

team in a new way. Welcome to a better way of leading: The Coach Approach.

WHAT IS COACHING?

Keith Webb, the founder of Creative Results Management, a firm that trains coaches, defines coaching this way:

> "COACHING INVOLVES LISTENING TO OTHERS, ASKING QUESTIONS TO DEEPEN THINKING, ALLOWING OTHERS TO FIND THEIR OWN SOLUTIONS, AND DOING IT ALL IN A WAY THAT MAKES PEOPLE FEEL EMPOWERED AND RESPONSIBLE ENOUGH TO TAKE ACTION."

I love that definition. In this book, we will be taking a deeper dive into each of the concepts listed above, but read that sentence again. Slowly! Digest what is being said. Here's what jumps out at me.

Listening—Admit it, most of us are poor listeners. For starters, we can be very distracted by our phones. Our phones often lead to thoughts racing through our minds.

I just got a text. How should I respond?
I wonder what they are thinking.
Did I reply to the last text?
I am hungry; what is for lunch?
Why did I wear this outfit? I don't even like it.

You get the point.

But good coaching depends on good listening. **Without listening well, we won't be able to ask good questions.** Good questions come when we pay attention to the challenges being shared. If we are not listening, how can we be curious? How can we be empathetic? How can we come alongside our team? **Listening is the beginning of coaching.** If we don't listen well, we don't begin well.

Asking Questions—If you get anything out of this book, I hope you become great at asking questions. Begin to evaluate not only your own questions, but questions other people are asking too. Listen to what's asked through one-on-one conversations and in groups. Start observing how people on TV ask and answer questions, or when you go to a speaking engagement and the speaker asks the audience a question. This will begin to sharpen your skills in asking great questions. Not all questions are great questions, though, which we will discuss later. **We need to become students of great questions.**

Deep Thinking—Allow yourself to be curious, allow yourself to be creative, and move outside the box of your personal experiences to explore new ways and new options. **The Coach Approach requires deep thinking.**

Find Their Own Solutions—This is important for you to grasp as a leader. Allowing your people to find their own solutions is a game-changer. It will help them own the solutions and the action steps they need to make a difference. This leads to more responsibility on their part. **They will take on the responsibility if they find the solution.**

Feeling Empowered—Think about a time when your supervisor asked you to give input, maybe they asked you a question looking for a solution. How did you feel? You probably felt like a million bucks. You might have been shocked that your boss, your supervisor, or maybe even your supervisor's supervisor asked you a question. Feeling empowered is thrilling.

What is The Coach Approach? The Coach Approach is a leadership style that is focused on using coaching principles to guide and manage other people. The Coach Approach is for anyone who is leading others as a staff person, volunteer organization, sports team, or even in a family. These principles will all apply.

A benefit of the Coach Approach is that teammates stay around longer when they feel they are empowered and valued. Empowered people repeat what they've experienced, and they go on to lead others in an empowering way. With an open mind and an open heart, let's dive into The Coach Approach: A better way to lead in business and beyond.

Note: This book is designed for anyone who is leading others as a staff person, volunteer organization, sports team or even in a family. These principles will all apply. The person you are coaching could be called coachee, client, or many other titles; but we will call them '**talent**' throughout this book. For businesses, sports, ministries, and other contexts, talent is an all-encompassing positive word. Since this book is focused on those leading others vs. certified coaches, we will refer to that person throughout the book as '**leader.**'

POSSIBILITIES

PART 1

POSSIBILITIES

> "A LEADER'S JOB IS NOT TO DO THE WORK
> FOR OTHERS; IT'S TO HELP OTHERS FIGURE
> OUT HOW TO DO IT THEMSELVES, TO GET
> THINGS DONE, AND TO SUCCEED BEYOND
> WHAT THEY THOUGHT POSSIBLE."
>
> – SIMON SINEK –

The Coach Approach begins with a possibility mindset and attitude. It's going to a place we didn't know or think we could go. It's where inventions and new ideas are birthed. This is out-of-the-box thinking, exploring options we haven't thought of, and going to places we have never been. Exploring the possibilities, engaging the head and heart, this is a whole new way of leading.

CHAPTER 1

GROWTH MINDSET VS. FIXED MINDSET

In Dr. Carol Dweck's book *Mindset: Changing the Way You Think to Fulfill Your Potential*, she masterfully helps the reader think differently by laying out the two mindsets people have: Growth Mindset and Fixed Mindset.

Additionally, she challenges others to use the power of rewarding effort and praising wisdom. Mindset coaches, like Dr. Dweck, help people break through their limited beliefs. And we ALL have limited beliefs. But, our possibilities are limited when we have fixed mindsets. As leaders, we need to enter conversations with growth mindsets and be open to new possibilities.

GROWTH MINDSET	FIXED MINDSET
Failure is an *opportunity* to grow.	Failure is the *limit* of my abilities.
I can learn to do *anything* I want.	I am *either* good at it or I'm not.
Challenges help me *grow*.	My abilities are *unchanging*.
I *like* to try new things.	I *stick* to what I know.
Feedback is *constructive*.	Feedback and criticism are *personal*.
I am *inspired* by the success of others.	When I am frustrated, I *give up*.
My effort and attitude *determine* my abilities.	My potential is *predetermined*.

HE COULDN'T SEE IT

Sometimes in life, because of our own limiting beliefs or because of others' limiting beliefs about us, we can't break out of our shells, or we have a difficult time doing something new or different.

In 1990, I found myself working full-time at a Methodist church and in the process of becoming an ordained Methodist pastor. Since I had many years of experience coaching high school wrestling, my senior pastor asked me to lead the charge and start up a sports ministry in our church. I knew it was a great fit, and I was truly excited for the opportunity. I began to read, research, and go to conferences to learn all I could about sports ministries.

Meanwhile, I was also filling out paperwork and taking psychological tests for my ordination process. When I came to the final stages of the evaluation, I met with a psychiatrist to discuss how I might fit into the role of pastor. I couldn't wait to finalize this process and begin my formal education in ministry. During the meeting, the psychiatrist affirmed many of my positive attributes, but then concluded that I would not be a good fit as a pastor because my passion was for sports ministry. He had never heard of such a thing, and he didn't think it was possible to have sports ministry happen inside the church (even though I told him stories of how we were already doing it).

At that moment, the opportunity of becoming a Methodist pastor ended. Just like that! But thank God, I didn't stop there. I kept learning, growing, and executing sports ministry. Here I am 30 years later, working full-time for the Fellowship of Christian Athletes, one of the largest sports ministries in the world. I am also an international leader for FCA. I have been to over 20 countries to train pastors and volunteers on how they can use the platform of sports to reach their communities.

The church psychiatrist did not see the possibilities; he had a fixed mindset. Because of that, the opportunity ended there. But fortunately, God had given me a growth mindset, and I saw the possibilities in sports ministry. I didn't give up, and I moved forward. God's blessed my life and the lives of others, and it taught me a valuable leadership lesson.

The mindset of the leader is to be curious, to look inside the heart of the talent, and to realize the potential for possibilities they've not previously experienced. As leaders, we need to help our talent see new possibilities that lie beyond the struggles or pain points in front of them. We shouldn't simply shut them down because something's never been done.

As leaders, we need to be sure we have adopted a growth mindset for ourselves and our talent. This is crucial to implementing the Coach Approach. We have to go into conversations with an open mind, a possibility mindset, and remember the power of "yet," it will happen at some point.

HIS MIND WAS SET

Recently, a friend called to share that his church had just built a gymnasium. He knew that in prior years, I led a thriving sports ministry in my church and he wanted to pick my brain. Hoping to engage him from the beginning, he included his pastor on the call. After they shared what they had completed at their church, my initial reaction was overwhelming excitement for their potential ministry opportunities. I wanted to share all my experience and knowledge.

But I held back, wanting to apply the Coach Approach to the conversation and ask questions instead of giving insight and answers.

As they shared, I could hear their excitement about the new building, but their ideas and possibilities for using it were limited. So I began to ask questions about how the community and the church could use it. Almost all my questions were shot down.

This was a challenge. The short conversation ended, and we went our separate ways. Even today, I am unsure of what resulted from our conversation.

After the call, I had to look myself in the mirror and ask myself if I asked good questions. I felt like I had listened well and posed thought-provoking questions. I then realized it came down to a fixed mindset versus a growth mindset. They seemed to be stuck, unable to see the relevance of my questions.

I humbly admit that due to my limited time, I was unable to help them think with a growth mindset and get unstuck. If I had more time, which I definitely needed, I would have asked more pointed questions to help them think deeper. Maybe some questions like: Do you really want strangers using your church? What would be a dream scenario for the use of this gym? Have you thought about the children, youth, and senior citizens in the community who could use it? These types of questions would have kept with the Coach Approach, and I could have helped them shift from a fixed mindset to a growth mindset that sees new opportunities and possibilities.

A big role of leaders is helping talent go from limited mindsets to growth mindsets. When they do, they will see more possibilities. These postures of the mind will drive people to see more possibilities. **And a possibilities mindset is crucial for a leader to help the talent.**

WISDOM FROM OTHERS

"Nothing is impossible. The word itself says, 'I'm possible."

– Audrey Hepburn –

"It's kind of fun to do the impossible."

– Walt Disney –

"Everything you want is on the other side of fear."

– Jack Canfield –

WISDOM FROM THE WORD

"Jesus said to him, 'If you can?' Everything
is possible for the one who believes."

– Mark 9:23 (CSB) –

"I planted, Apollos watered, but God gave the growth."

– 1 Corinthians 3:6 (CSB) –

"His divine power has given us everything required
for life and godliness through the knowledge of him
who called us by his own glory and goodness."

– 2 Peter 1:3 (CSB) –

TIME FOR ACTION

Reflect on the things you are doing well with a growth vs. fixed mindset.

_____

_____

_____

Reflect on what you need to change with a growth vs. fixed mindset.

_____

_____

_____

What is a powerful question you want to ask yourself as a leader regarding helping your talent identify their mindsets?

_____

_____

_____

Based on what you learned in this chapter, complete this sentence:

I will _____

_____

CHAPTER 2

BELIEVE SOMETHING DIFFERENT IS POSSIBLE

"What is the number one thing you hate about your job?" I asked Lucy, the hiring manager.

"Annual reviews," she said.

"Why the annual reviews?"

"I hate telling people they are wrong."

"I wonder what it would look like for you not to hate annual reviews."

"Well, I have been doing these for 30 years. Nothing has changed. They are just hard to do and will always be."

Of course, I wanted to tell her all I knew about annual reviews and my experience with them. In my leadership roles, I have led many annual reviews with over 100 people but I realized that I wouldn't be using the Coach Approach. There's a better way, so I began asking more questions.

"What is the part you hate the most about annual reviews?"

"Telling them where they are weak," she replied.

"Do you think they know where they're weak already?"

"Yes, probably," she said. "Most people know their weaknesses already, which is one of the reasons they don't like reviews. They do not like hearing what they already know."

Her reasoning made sense, but I kept pressing her.

"If you know where they're weak, and they know where they're weak, but you don't want to tell them, how else could this come to light?"

She thought for a minute and I waited patiently. Silence was golden at this moment. She finally said, "I don't know."

So, I took a different angle: "Who leads the annual review?"

"I do," she replied.

"What if you let them lead the annual review?"

She pondered this, considering the risk versus reward. I could see the tension leave her face and her shoulders relax as she contemplated this new discovery.

"They would probably tell me their weaknesses and I wouldn't have to tell them."

The Coach Approach made her think and it led to something different.

Lucy became excited to host annual reviews because of a different perspective. She came up with a new process. She gave her employees questions to answer in advance of their reviews, and they came prepared. The new approach reduced the tension on both her side and her talent's side. When she reviewed the employees' answers, she realized they already knew 80% of their weaknesses and she only needed to discuss the small percentage of weaknesses for which they were unaware. This allowed her to spend more time encouraging, cheering, and congratulating them in their strong areas. The Coach Approach led her and her team to a better way and to something different.

GRABBERS OF THE IMPOSSIBLE

When leading others, it's a huge challenge to get them to believe something different is possible when we have never experienced it ourselves. It is out of the realm of what we have seen. The Coach Approach challenges us to be explorers of what we have never seen before alongside our talent. We do this by believing and having no fear of asking any question.

The Coach Approach is ok with failure because we have a growth mindset and failure is really learning to get us to the impossible. **Belief is the door to the impossible.**

CT Studd was a missionary to China and Africa. He said, "God is not looking for the nibblers of the possible, but the grabbers of the impossible." CT Studd, unlike most missionaries that came from low- to middle-class families, came from great wealth. He had seen the possibility with wealth, but he wanted to see the impossible that could only be done with Christ.

Belief is what will cause people to reach for something impossible and make it possible. Lack of belief is a roadblock. Leaders must be positive and keep a mindset of believing in possibilities.

It's critical for leaders to believe these two things:

One, you have to believe in the talent you are coaching. It will be virtually impossible to help them experience a breakthrough when they are stuck if you don't believe they can do it.

Two, you need a "can do" attitude that makes all impossible things possible. Persevere when things feel impossible, and stay positive. Believe that change can happen.

LETTING GO

One leader I began coaching relayed that he was working long hours and that he felt overwhelmed with all the work in front of him. I asked him to tell me more about the work he was doing. He said he spent a good portion of his day checking tickets from production for accuracy before they were submitted. My first question in response was if one of his staff members could look them over. He said it was quite technical and took some experience, and he wasn't sure they would have the time. Going deeper, I asked him to tell me one or two important skills needed to look over the tickets. One of them was to have an eagle eye. He said between 6 and 20 tickets needed processing each day, and each one required one to five minutes to review. I offered that maybe he could give the one-minute tickets to someone else with an eagle eye. But he was not comfortable with that suggestion. He didn't believe anyone else had the needed skills.

The Coach Approach made it painfully obvious that the talent's core issue was unbelief. He didn't believe someone else could do the job, so he refused to relinquish it. Holding onto this job with the tickets prevented him from leading others, which was his main responsibility. To me, there was something deeper going on. Something deeper than the bottom line and finances. He didn't believe in his staff, and he couldn't give away the responsibility. It wasn't long before he was moved into a role with no one reporting to him since he had become a bottleneck in the growth of the company.

One of the great things about coaching is that it brings the root issues to the surface. Is the situation the manager says is the problem truly the problem? It might be, or it might be something they don't recognize that goes much deeper than what they're sharing. It's the leader's job to ask questions and discover the root of the issue. Oftentimes, it's tied to belief.

Leaders who take the Coach Approach will have to become pros at believing in new possibilities. The talent will follow your lead. If you can choose to see things differently, they'll follow your lead. Belief can take time, especially if you're changing beliefs, but don't give up. Sometimes motivation will show up in unexpected places.

I have traveled to Southeast Asia many times, and I love hearing the golden buddha story. In 1957, an entire monastery in Thailand was being relocated. When they began to move a huge buddha statue from the front of their temple, they realized there was a crack. As they began to look closer at the crack, they saw gold. One monk decided to chisel the crack out more, and they realized there was a golden buddha inside of the clay buddha statue.

As leaders, we must believe that even in the cracks, there can be gold, and this is what we coach our talent to believe too.

WISDOM FROM OTHERS

"Instead keep your eyes open and your head up. Be open to new possibilities. Be kind to people. Take action. Believe that something great is coming your way. Maintain hope. Believe in what's possible."

– Jon Gordon –

"Imagine what would happen if you decided to believe that you could."

– Jamie Kern Lima, Founder of IT Cosmetics –

"So many things are possible as long as you don't know they are impossible."

– Mildred D. Taylor, The Land –

WISDOM FROM THE WORD

"I am sure of this, that he who started a good work in you will carry it on to completion until the day of Christ Jesus. Indeed, it is right for me to think this way about all of you, because I have you in my heart, and you are all partners with me in grace, both in my imprisonment and in the defense and confirmation of the gospel. For God is my witness, how deeply I miss all of you with the affection of Christ Jesus."

– Philippians 1:6-8 (CSB) –

"Now may the God of hope fill you with all joy and peace in believing, so that you may overflow with hope by the power of the Holy Spirit."

– Romans 15: 13 (CSB) –

"I pray that the eyes of your heart may be enlightened so that you may know what is the hope of his calling, what is the wealth of his glorious inheritance in the saints, and what is the immeasurable greatness of his power toward us who believe, according to the mighty working of his strength."

– Ephesians 1:18-19 (CSB) –

TIME FOR ACTION

Reflect on the things you are doing well with believing in your talent.

_____

_____

_____

Reflect on the things you need to change with believing in your talent.

_____

_____

_____

What is a powerful question you want to ask yourself as a leader regarding believing in your talent?

_____

_____

_____

Based on what you learned in this chapter, complete this sentence:

I will _____

_____

CHAPTER 3

ACT DIFFERENTLY

> "IT'S EASIER TO JUST KEEP DOING WHAT WE
> HAVE BEEN DOING, RATHER THAN DOING
> THE THINGS NECESSARY TO CHANGE."
>
> – KEITH WEBB –

It's easy to say but hard to do. Changing our actions and behaviors is hard. The Coach Approach will challenge even the best of leaders to act differently. But, it's worth it.

For many reasons, I believe it's time for leaders to consider how to lead in a different way. Society alone is leading many of us to act differently.

WORKPLACE CHANGES

More than ever before, thanks in part to the pandemic, many of us are living and working in a virtual world. Getting the job done at home has become routine for many, but working remotely comes with its own challenges and opportunities. No one is popping into your office down the hall or making a pitstop at the break room. Many of us have lost our connection. Because of that, we need to intentionally connect. But, as a whole, that is where we are seeing a breakdown.

Generational differences have become increasingly obvious as the world changes faster than it ever has before. Younger generations in the workplace want to explore opportunities and conclusions that may be different from other generations. Some see this as a problem, but leaders should see it as an opportunity.

The Coach Approach is very powerful in bridging generational differences because it helps people self-discover the new opportunities and new ways to serve and work together. It is a partnering way to accomplish work and goals versus the traditional top-down approach often found in the workplace.

GOOGLE TEACHES US TO MANAGE DIFFERENTLY

In June 2019, Inc.com posted a column by author and speaker Scott Mautz who talked about Google's attempt to act differently and prove that managers do not matter. During "Project Oxygen," as Google called it, they got rid of all management and leadership hierarchies. It was disastrous and the experiment didn't last long. But Google actually ended up discovering several traits of the very best managers. In the column, the first trait identified is that managers need to be good coaches.

Scott went on to explain that a good coach is not a fixer but a facilitator. Good facilitators listen well and ask great questions. Good coaches truly care about their people. It's difficult to inspire followership and make progress when you don't care about your talent. I love how Google and several other organizations came to this conclusion by being curious, which is one attribute that makes Google great. **These are two ways leaders need to act differently: be facilitators not fixers, and be leaders who care for their teammates and coach them well.**

SHOW THEM THEIR VALUE

Your people are your greatest asset. When you let this soak in, it should motivate you to act differently, be more intentional in listening, and raise your game in communicating. Communicating with them to bring out their best is essential. Dr. Brené Brown, a research professor who studies courage, vulnerability, shame, and empathy, says, "When people don't know their value, they're hustling for their worth." How are you going to show them you value them? How are you going to unlock their potential?

A great way to do that is to take the Coach Approach. Not only will it unlock potential and show people they are valued, but the results will be tremendous. Valued teammates lead to increased revenue and employee retention, and every business wants that! But valued teammates also mean increased fulfillment, stronger relationships, and higher satisfaction, things all organizations need to thrive. It is expensive to hire someone, onboard them, train them, and help them develop the relationships necessary for success. After all the hard work to hire and integrate a new hire, implement the Coach Approach to keep them fully engaged.

IT IS OK TO NOT KNOW THE ANSWER

One of the scary things about the Coach Approach is that you will have to act differently and be okay with not knowing the answer. Dr. Brené Brown also says, "We feel that we help by having answers—advice, do's and don'ts, knowledge. However, by admitting that we don't know—that we don't even know what to say—is a counterintuitive way to approach a situation that generates connection and brings us together…"

As you go and engage in conversations, you're naturally going to want to give the answer; but if you ask a question, you may get a very unexpected response. Even when you don't know where the conversation is going to go, you need to be okay with stepping into a coaching conversation with your talent. This leap allows you to explore more opportunities and ways to solve problems that your talent mentions, which often leads to new discoveries and new solutions.

CAN YOU "LEAD UP" WITH THE COACH APPROACH?

The focus of this book is helping leaders develop their teams. However, some have asked, "Can we 'lead up' with the Coach Approach?" The Coach Approach often leads people to listen, explore, and ask better questions, regardless of if they're the leader or the talent. However, the issue comes down to posture.

If your the talent and your leader is prideful, selfish, or knows it all, it will be much more difficult to take the Coach Approach with them. But if they are humble, selfless, and open to learning new ways, you may have an open door for conversation.

In either scenario, if you decide to ask questions that may challenge what your leader says, start by showing humility—ask permission to ask a question. Once you receive permission, begin with a clarifying question and move on from there to more challenging questions.

In order to "lead up," strongly consider the depth of the relationship. The depth factor will depend on how far you go and how challenging your questions can be. Another thing to consider is your leader's mindset: Do they consider themselves the top dog? Do they hold tight to their title of leader, executive, or president? If so, you will want to approach conversations carefully and respectfully.

Consider the posture of your supervisor and the strength of your relationship before stepping into the Coach Approach to "lead up."

VALUE RESULTS AND RELATIONSHIPS

In the business world, in nonprofits, and also in ministry, we can be driven by "results" and the pressure to grow. When we focus on results more than relationships, our team knows it and feels it. We have the choice to treat people and teammates as a transaction, or we can treat people like we really care for them. Believe me, teammates know whether you're using them for transactions or if you truly care about them.

The Coach Approach, which is a different way of having relationships, can help you lean into both results and relationships. Both are necessary for success, company growth, employee retention, positive morale, and for the feeling of being on an awesome team.

MICROMANAGERS WILL KILL YOUR SOUL

Micromanaging will kill a leader's soul and the souls of everyone they lead. If you're not sure if you're a micromanager, humbly ask your team. Staff absolutely know when their manager is a micromanager. Micromanagers do not naturally use the Coach Approach, and if this is you, you'll need to act differently starting today.

My wife and I were having a conversation with our long-lost friend, Cindy, and we asked her what she did for a living. She told us about her work, and we asked how she enjoyed her boss and her team. She said she recently had a change in supervisors. The new supervisor was a micromanager; and because of his style of leadership, she was about ready to quit. She described the experience of working under a micromanager well: "You're never right; you lose your confidence and ability to do tasks on your own, and it is a soul-killer."

Wow, powerful words from somebody about her unhealthy supervisor. Her story made me stop and reflect over my leadership. It should make all leaders pause and reflect.

What would your staff say about you? This is not a question to be glazed over, but one to really think about.

Am I a micromanager?
Am I creating fear in my staff by micromanaging?
And worst of all, am I a soul-killer by micromanaging?

To no surprise, Cindy didn't last long at her job. She decided to quit. Rightly so. I truly believe if her supervisor would have partnered with her in the Coach Approach, she would have stayed and excelled in her role. Her company would have retained her thousands of hours of experience, which would have only bettered them even more.

The Coach Approach starts by stretching us to consider new possibilities that we have never experienced before. The only way we can do that is to have a growth mindset, truly believe in our hearts that something different is possible, and act differently to execute the possibilities. Once we start there, we need to review our head and heart posture.

WISDOM FROM OTHERS

"I've made lots of mistakes. Probably the worst one—I would say they tie. It's either when I didn't move fast enough on something, or I didn't take a big enough risk."

– IBM CEO Ginni Rometty –

"If you always do what you always did, you will always get what you always got."

– Albert Einstein –

"Trying different ways of doing things is what brings invention."

– Unknown –

WISDOM FROM THE WORD

"Do nothing out of selfish ambition or vain conceit. Rather, in humility value others above yourselves, not looking to your own interests but each of you to the interests of the others."

– Philippians 2:3-4 (NIV) –

"Therefore, be imitators of God, as dearly loved children, and walk in love, as Christ also loved us and gave himself for us, a sacrificial and fragrant offering to God."

– Ephesians 5:1-2 (CSB) –

"Now if any of you lacks wisdom, he should ask God—who gives to all generously and ungrudgingly—and it will be given to him."

– James 1:5 (CSB) –

TIME FOR ACTION

Reflect on the things you need to change to "act differently."

_____

_____

_____

What do you anticipate will be the hardest behavior to change regarding "act differently?"

_____

_____

_____

What is a powerful question you want to ask yourself as a leader regarding "act differently?"

_____

_____

_____

Based on what you learned in this chapter, complete this sentence:

I will _____

_____

POSTURE

PART 2

POSTURE

THE POSTURE OF A GREAT COACH

To take the Coach Approach, being open to possibilities isn't enough. You need to enter conversations with the right posture in both your head and your heart. Stopping to take an honest assessment of yourself is critical. Others will not receive your coaching to its fullness if you don't keep the right posture. You may find the need to make some changes right from the start.

POSTURE: HEAD

CHAPTER 4

CURIOUS

> "REMEMBER THAT THINGS ARE NOT ALWAYS AS THEY APPEAR TO BE... CURIOSITY CREATES POSSIBILITIES AND OPPORTUNITIES."
>
> – ROY T. BENNETT –

PASSIONATELY CURIOUS

I love this quote by a brilliant man, Albert Einstein: "I have no special talent. I am only passionately curious."

As a leader, manager, and influencer, you probably have the answers, or most of the answers to the questions your staff are asking you. That is not a bad thing, but knowledge is the biggest inhibitor of curiosity.

In some ways, we have lost the art of curiosity because we have Google. If we need an answer, we simply do a quick online search to find it. But curiosity is truly thought provoking. As leaders, we must reclaim it.

In business, our role is to ask questions such as: What are the solutions to the problems we have? In ministry, we need to ask questions like: What are the roadblocks to enhancing and expanding the ministry? Unless we approach our problems with curiosity, we won't find solutions. Being curious is a part of the Coach Approach that will cause us to look at problems from different angles.

We can develop our curiosity by expanding the questions we ask. What are some of the broad areas of angles to ask questions?

1. Questions about the past
2. Questions about the future
3. Questions probing into their emotions
4. Questions probing into their heart

See the final section of the book for Pro Tips on angle questions.

CURIOSITY LEADS TO SUCCESS

"What qualities do you see most often in those who succeed?" Adam Bryant asked over 700 CEOs he interviewed for his book, *Corner Office.*

The number one answer on their lists: Curiosity.

Wow, curiosity? This has to make you and me pause. Is that what you would have said? Why not leadership, charisma, or time management? There must be something about curiosity we need to take note of.

"How does curiosity lead to success? Curiosity pushes people toward uncertainty and allows them to approach it with a positive attitude. Curiosity is not only linked to success because it leads to creativity and discoveries. It also helps you develop meaningful relationships that enrich your personal and professional life." (Kortivity.com blog)

A BEGINNER'S MINDSET

> "WE NEED TO RECLAIM THE BEGINNER'S MIND."
>
> **– YO-YO MA –**
> FAMOUS CELLIST

Remember when you didn't know? Maybe you didn't know what someone was talking to you about, or you were unfamiliar with something. Remember when you were a beginner at... you name it. Curiosity drove you to begin to learn more. For beginners to grow, they have to be curious. As a leader, you'll need to be curious and keep a beginner's mindset when working with your talent.

Someone with a beginner's mindset will:

1. Be open-minded. They are willing to learn and relearn or start fresh with the challenges brought to them. Let yourself move into wonder.
2. Be relentless at asking questions. Questions help us learn more and also feed our curiosity.
3. Be unwilling to accept things at face value. In our minds, we can't say, "I know that," or "That is impossible," because

it's never been done before. We have to think maybe there is more here. You're like a detective that comes to your crime scene, and you're curious. You have experience in these types of crime scenes, yet you don't totally know what may have happened. This is the type of curiosity you need.

4. Be willing to be an active listener versus a passive listener. An active listener is on their A-game and fully engaged.
5. **Be willing to step into the unknown. The unknown is where curiosity leads you.**
6. Be willing to be comfortable with the uncomfortable. Being curious is being willing to be silent and allowing yourself to wrestle with questions. Be comfortable with silence; this is where people can dive deeper into curiosity.

WISDOM FROM OTHERS

"Don't let anyone rob you of your imagination, your creativity, or your curiosity. It's your place in the world; it's your life. Go on and do all you can with it, and make it the life you want to live."

– Mae Jemison, First African American Woman Astronaut in Space –

"The important thing is not to stop questioning… Never lose a holy curiosity."

– Albert Einstein –

"We keep moving forward, opening new doors, and doing new things, because we're curious; and curiosity keeps leading us down new paths."

– Walt Disney –

WISDOM FROM THE WORD

"They took him and brought him to the Areopagus, and said, 'May we learn about this new teaching you are presenting? Because what you say sounds strange to us, and we want to know what these things mean.' Now all the Athenians and the foreigners residing there spent their time on nothing else but telling or hearing something new."

– Acts 17:19-21 (CSB) –

"It is the glory of God to conceal a matter and the glory of kings to investigate a matter."

– Proverbs 25:2 (CSB) –

"All things are wearisome, more than anyone can say. The eye is not satisfied by seeing or the ear filled with hearing."

– Ecclesiastes 1:8 (CSB) –

TIME FOR ACTION

Reflect on the ways you are doing well with curiosity with your talent.

_____

_____

_____

Reflect on the ways you need to change to be more curious.

_____

_____

_____

What is a powerful question you want to ask yourself as a leader regarding curiosity?

_____

_____

_____

Based on what you learned in this chapter, complete this sentence:

I will _____

_____

CHAPTER 5

ACTIVE LISTENING

> "THE BEGINNING OF LOVE FOR THE BRETHREN IS
> LEARNING TO LISTEN TO THEM... MANY PEOPLE
> ARE LOOKING FOR AN EAR THAT WILL LISTEN."
>
> – DIETRICH BONHOEFFER –

Listening is at the core of the Coach Approach. We must listen. We have so much noise in our lives, so much competing for our attention, that it can often be hard to listen. Do you think you listen well? Or do you just wait for your turn to talk? Are you fully present when you are listening? When we are trying to help our talent with the Coach Approach, sometimes all we need to do is listen well.

In full transparency, I must confess that while I was a student at Salisbury State College, now called Salisbury University in Maryland, I took a communication class titled Listening. I'm embarrassed to say my grade. Should I really share what I earned in that class? Okay, so I got a C in listening. How embarrassing is that, especially for someone like myself, who is now a leadership coach? I would like to say I have improved to a C+, but my wife and four daughters might still give me a C, maybe even a C-. I know I am a poor listener, and I need to continue to improve. I am currently listening to a podcast on how to get better at listening. I'd say that's a step in the right direction!

LISTENING TAKES WORK

Think about it. Listening is something that we do (or should do) a lot every single day. Really every hour. Every meeting. Every phone call. Every interaction. Aren't those reasons convincing enough for you and me to stop and say enough is enough. Now is the time for us to improve as listeners. I will be a better supervisor, leader, coach, spouse, parent, son, friend, or volunteer if I can put my own desires and distractions aside for a time to be present when listening.

Have you ever asked yourself, "Why is it so hard to be a good listener?" I know I've asked myself that many times. Honestly, most people are not good listeners. I think even the ones who appear to be good listeners still struggle with thinking about other thoughts and conversations outside of the one in front of them.

What are the issues when it comes to listening? We are distracted. By what? Several things.

1. Our phones. We know it. We hear people talk about how our phones are distracting us all the time. Pastors preach about it during sermons. My coaching colleagues warn us about it. My work teammates bring it up. Last night

my wife addressed it. "Are you listening to me?" she asked. My reply was yes, but in truth, I was half listening and half typing a text.

2. Thoughts in our minds. Our thoughts can be distracting! Thoughts from a previous conversation, from a struggle we're dealing with, or thoughts about the next meeting. All kinds of things race through our minds, and they are distracting us from listening well.

3. The activity around us. Someone walks by the cubicle while we're trying to pay attention and listen. We're having a meeting in the local coffee shop where lots of activity is going on, and we become distracted. We may even be distracted by nontangibles like the temperature in the room.

4. The things closest to us. The mess on our desks or the stack of papers we need to get to, and yet we're trying to be a good listener.

All of us are constantly surrounded by so many distractions, it's no wonder it's hard for you and me to be good listeners. To be the focused listener our colleagues and friends deserve, it will take intentional focus and change.

BECOMING A BETTER LISTENER

What are some of the solutions to overcome common struggles with listening? This is not rocket science. This is not even new to you and me. We need to be intentional about becoming a better listener. Here's how:

1. Silence the phone and put it down when you are trying to be an active listener. Sometimes I do this, but there is still something (maybe an addiction, a need to please) that makes me want to pick it up. I have found that sometimes, I need to put the phone out of sight. Some of us need to turn off notifications on our smart watches too.

2. As thoughts pop in your mind that have nothing to do with the conversation in front of you, write them down on a little piece of paper so you can refocus on being a powerful listener.

3. Move yourself or your seat to a position where you will not be distracted during the conversation. Maybe you need to choose a seat where you're facing the wall, not people. I am an extrovert. My preferred seat in a restaurant is my back to the wall and facing all the action and people in the restaurant. Yet, that is the worst seat for me if I want to be a powerful listener. Maybe you need to take the conversation in the cubicle and move it to a private meeting room with your back to the window and all the traffic in the hallway.

4. Turn off all notifications on your laptop. I have recently started to use the *do not disturb* toggle on my laptop and phone. It works great. Straighten up your desk before your conversation so you're not distracted by the paper piles you need to deal with later on.

ACTIVE LISTENING

The training from ICF has really helped me understand and become a better listener. To be great at listening, you must focus on active listening.

The International Coaching Federation (ICF) has this to say about listening:

"Active Listening—Ability to focus completely on what the client is saying and is not saying, to understand the meaning of what is said in the context of the client's desires, and to support client self-expression.

1. Distinguishes between the words, the tone of voice, and the body language.
2. Summarizes, paraphrases, reiterates, and mirrors back what client has said to ensure clarity and understanding.
3. Integrates and builds on client's ideas and suggestions.
4. "Bottom-lines" or understands the essence of the client's communication and helps the client get there rather than engaging in long, descriptive stories.
5. Allows the client to vent or "clear" the situation without judgment or attachment in order to move on to next steps."

ARE YOU HEARING WHAT IS NOT BEING SAID?

Have you heard of the 93/7 rule?

> "93% OF COMMUNICATION OCCURS THROUGH
> NONVERBAL BEHAVIOR AND TONE;
> ONLY 7% OF COMMUNICATION TAKES
> PLACE THROUGH THE USE OF WORDS."
>
> – JOHN STOKER –

Whether you agree with the numbers or not, a high percentage of communication is nonverbal. As you coach, you must be attentive and be aware of what is not being verbalized.

As you can imagine, listening is so much more than hearing what somebody says and parroting back to them what you just heard. You and your talent both have filters that make listening even harder. Some of the filters are: culture, values, beliefs, language, attitudes, expectations, and intentions. Being a powerful listener can be a huge challenge.

Also, we need to listen for what our talent is not saying, their nonverbal cues. Back in my college days, I also took a class on nonverbal communication. I'm happy to say I did a lot better in that class compared to the listening class. When you're listening, you have to be in touch with the tone of voice, body posture, eyes, and anything else the talent is using to communicate outside of words. Listening this way engages you at a deeper level, allowing you to follow up with a better question or maybe even a challenging question. Some of those questions might be:

1. Is there a deeper meaning here?
2. Can you tell me more?
3. What question would your spouse, supervisor, or coworker ask you about this?

RASA

There is a lot written about different levels of listening and ways to improve.

RASA — is an acronym by Julian Edwards that stands for: Receive, Appreciate, Summarize, and Ask.

"**R**eceive: Is what the person saying including what they are not saying?

Appreciate: Affirm them and what they are saying.

Summarize: Condense what they said including the key points and share a brief summary.

Ask: Follow up what they said with a thought-provoking question."

LISTENING LEVELS

As you begin to grow in the area of listening, it will be helpful to know your level of listening in any given conversation. I have found these four listening levels to be helpful:

1. **Pretend:** Our mind and mental energy is somewhere else. You are at a meeting, and physically you are present,

but mentally you are not. This is easy to do anywhere, but especially on a video meeting.

2 **Partial:** You get pieces, but not the full picture. Similar to the pretend level, being online for training or a webinar, it is very easy to be a partial listener.

3. **Present:** You did some work to minimize distractions. Effort was taken to improve your possibility of learning more.

4. **Powerful:** You hear more in depth. Their values, what motivates them, and listening for what is not being said. More focus, less distractions.

The bottom line is that listening is work. We must put in the work to improve our listening. **As a leader, if you are listening well, you are leading well.**

WISDOM FROM OTHERS

"It's hard to listen when you are talking or when you are thinking of a response."

– Catherine Pulsifer –

"Most people do not listen with the intent to understand; they listen with the intent to reply."

– Stephen Covey –

"Improving your listening is a daily ritual – a commitment to make progress in every discussion, phone call, and meeting. Making an improvement to your listening takes a moment to decide and a lifetime of practice to master."

– Oscar Trimboli, author, host of the Apple award-winning podcast *Deep Listening* –

WISDOM FROM THE WORD

"When words are many, transgression is not lacking,
but whoever restrains his lips is prudent."

– Proverbs 10:19 (ESV) –

"My dear brothers and sisters, understand this: Everyone
should be quick to listen, slow to speak, and slow to anger,"

– James 1:19 (CSB) –

"A fool's way is right in his own eyes, but
whoever listens to counsel is wise."

– Proverbs 12:15 (CSB) –

THE COACH APPROACH

TIME FOR ACTION

Reflect on the things you are doing well when it comes
to listening.

_____

_____

_____

Reflect on the things you need to change to become a
better listener.

_____

_____

_____

What is a powerful question you want to ask yourself as a leader
regarding listening?

_____

_____

_____

Based on what you learned in this chapter, complete this
sentence:

I will _____

_____

CHAPTER 6

THINK DIFFERENTLY

> "AS A LEADER, YOU DON'T HAVE TO HAVE ALL THE ANSWERS. IN FACT, HAVING THE ANSWERS IS LESS IMPORTANT THAN ASKING GOOD QUESTIONS."
>
> – MICHAEL HYATT –

Different can be uncomfortable. As leaders, people come to us and expect us to know the answers to their questions. As leaders, we expect to have all the answers. To begin the process of thinking differently, we need to get comfortable with the uncomfortable. The Coach Approach for you may feel foreign. And foreign is almost always uncomfortable.

If you want to be an effective leader, you will need to be willing to take the harder road. I truly believe the Coach Approach is the harder way, but it is the better way, with better results. So when you shift your mindset from being a teller to a leader, it will be harder, because telling is easier. Telling is the way you have always done it. But, it's time to think differently.

W.A.I.T. — WHY AM I TALKING?

Sometimes we need to pause and think, and maybe ask ourselves the question: Why am I talking? Some of us, myself included, are talkers. That is our natural DNA. There are talkers who have the self-awareness that they are talkers, and they have the self-control to manage over-talking. Unfortunately, there are talkers who are not self-aware and don't have the self-control to manage their over-talking. Some of us have the benefit of having a spouse or close friend who gives us the signal to stop talking when we've said too much.

Are you more of a talker than a listener?

Talkers love to step in to solve problems. Maybe worse is talkers are prideful and believe they have the best answers. But talkers need to be patient and curious, they need to let the talent sit in their situation for a bit without offering their two cents.

Begin to wait more during conversations and apply the concept of W.A.I.T. (Why am I talking). This will help you listen more and talk less.

AM I AN ADVICE MONSTER?

Would your staff say you are an Advice Monster? Michael Bungay Stanier uses this term in his TedX talk. Advice is not bad; but when we become an Advice Monster, we are not leading well, and we are definitely not leading with the Coach Approach.

You may say, "But I am an expert in this field, and my staff are rookies. I should lavish them with all my wisdom." You may need to check your pride too. Here are a few problems with being an Advice Monster:

1. You may be solving the wrong problem or challenge. Advice Monsters are often the opposite of active listeners. Because they don't take the time to listen, they may end up solving the wrong problem. They will not truly understand the real challenge, because they were so excited to share all their knowledge.

2. Your advice is not as good as you think. That might be hard to hear, but this is a pride issue. There is no place for pride in the Coach Approach. Too often, we come into conversations and to meetings pounding our chests. Look at ME, I have all the answers! Be careful, you may not be as good as you think you are. Right now you may be thinking about a ME Monster you work with, but I challenge you to look in the mirror first.

3. It can be poor leadership. By being an Advice Monster, you are saying, "My talent can't solve these issues." Your talent needs you to lead them well and help them find the solutions to their issues, not offer endless advice.

WE HAVE TO MOVE

> ACCORDING TO A STANFORD UNIVERSITY STUDY, "A PERSON'S CREATIVE OUTPUT INCREASED BY 60% WHEN THEY WERE WALKING. A GREAT REASON TO GET UP AND GO!"

The Stanford study also made it clear that actions impact our minds. Going for a walk, getting outside, and changing our environment will impact how we think. To apply the Coach Approach and think differently, make sure some type of movement is a part of your day.

Some of you may have a regular exercise regime. Others may do something as simple as a 10-minute walk during the day. I love taking a phone call while walking, especially if I am going to be on a long call. Working on the physical side of ourselves will impact our thinking too.

MINDSET

You may have heard the phrase, "If you can't do it right, don't do it at all." It's a popular phrase many parents teach their children. Generally, we are taught that if we're going to do something, do it the best we can, with excellence.

While these may be good tools for parenting, as leaders who are coaching a talent, we need to shift our focus. We cannot encourage our talent to wait for perfection before they try something. As a leader, you cannot wait for perfection before you try something. Take it easy on yourself and be willing to learn new skills and think differently. I would encourage you to take one aspect of coaching, maybe listening or asking questions, and work to be really good at one of those. As you challenge your thinking, I would like for you to consider:

- Am I willing to be great at asking questions versus giving answers?
- Am I willing to work at being great at listening versus telling?
- Am I willing to consider that self-discovery for my talent could be more powerful than my telling them what to do?

In the beginning, adopt a learner mindset and remind yourself with the power of 'yet.' I am not **yet** the leader I want to be, but I am on my way! I am a continual learner and strive to lead my teammates well.

WISDOM FROM OTHERS

"If you change the way you look at things,
the things you look at change."

– Wayne Dwyer –

"If everyone is thinking alike, then someone isn't thinking."

– George S. Patton –

"Be brave enough to think differently and
courageous enough to do the undoable or
unthinkable… To achieve the unachievable."

– Venkat Desireddy –

WISDOM FROM THE WORD

"for it's like someone calculating inwardly. 'Eat and drink,' he says to you, but his heart is not with you."

– Proverbs 23:7 (CSB) –

"Do not be conformed to this age, but be transformed by the renewing of your mind, so that you may discern what is the good, pleasing, and perfect will of God."

– Romans 12:2 (CSB) –

"I will meditate on your precepts and think about your ways."

– Psalm 119:15 (CSB) –

TIME FOR ACTION

Reflect on the things you are doing well regarding thinking differently.

_____

_____

_____

Reflect on the things you need to change to think differently.

_____

_____

_____

What is a powerful question you want to ask yourself as a leader regarding thinking differently?

_____

_____

_____

Based on what you learned in this chapter, complete this sentence:

I will _____

_____

POSTURE: HEART

CHAPTER 7

HUMBLE / WANTING THE BEST FOR OTHERS

For most of you, you have risen to the role you are in, with the title you have, because of your knowledge. You have probably been telling people what to do and answering questions throughout your whole career. Because of that, you may feel pretty darn good about yourself. You might not call yourself prideful, but others might. I love what C.S. Lewis says about being humble, "It is not thinking less of yourself but thinking of yourself less."

For many reasons, you are going to want to blurt out the answer(s) while you lead because it is what you have always done, and because it is the quickest way to solve the issue and move on. But you need to clothe yourself with humility and think about what is best for your talent.

The Bible admonishes us to do this in Colossians 3:12, "Therefore, as God's chosen ones, holy and dearly loved, put on compassion, kindness, humility, gentleness, and patience." What would it look like to put on humility in each conversation with your staff?

The heart posture of humility allows the talent to explore possibilities, new avenues, and out-of-the-box thinking.

Delta CEO, Ed Bastian, shared some of the best advice he has ever received: "Humility is essential for leadership." That is powerful advice embraced by a CEO of over 75,000 employees. You are reading this book because you are a leader. Truly embracing humility as a posture of your heart is key to implementing the Coach Approach.

EDGING GOD OUT

Leadership guru, Ken Blanchard, reminds us that, "The greatest barrier to leading like Jesus is *Edging God Out* (EGO) of our lives." Ken provides clarity, using E.G.O. as an acronym for Edge God Out, so we can identify when we're making it more about us and our egos versus God.

Ken says, "We believe we can Edge God Out in three ways: you can replace Him as the object of your worship; as the source of your security, self-worth, and wisdom; and as the audience for and authority over your daily work and life story."

The opposite of living with humility is living with a big ego.

As a Christian who coaches on a regular basis, I pray before each opportunity to coach with this ancient prayer: "Come, Holy Spirit come." I don't want to Edge God Out; I want to do just the opposite and humble myself before my Creator and invite Him in to lead and guide the conversation.

Good leaders using the Coach Approach self-reflect about where and how they Edge God Out in conversations and work to change that.

DOING HUMBLE THINGS

One of my favorite authors is Patrick Lencioni, who wrote one of the most useful books I've ever read called: "The Ideal Team Player: How to Recognize and Cultivate the Three Essential Virtues." He shares what he has found are the three most important attributes of any teammate. He looks to hire people who are humble, hungry, and smart (people smart).

It is very hard to teach humility, but I believe Kristen Kern does a nice job giving some ways we can live that can develop humility in us.

"Humility, unfortunately, is something that's difficult to teach, but I have seen leaders with true discipline have success in showing up more humbly by mimicking certain behaviors long enough that they become second nature.

This means doing humble things like:

- complimenting teammates
- readily admitting mistakes
- sharing credit with the team
- offering and accepting apologies
- accepting accountability with grace
- showing conviction with openness
- listening to input of others
- inviting open debate from the team"

* written by Kristine Kern, *The Marker of a Humble Leader*

As I was writing this chapter on humility, I was thinking that I wanted to be more humble. But the driver, Type-A personality in me wants to "work" at being more humble. Being humble is about my attitude and heart posture; and for me, it is also about considering others first. Following Kristine's list of suggestions, repeated over time, will develop us into humble leaders.

WANTING THE BEST FOR OTHERS

Wanting the best for others is another sign of humility. You may assume that you always want the best for others, but I have found that is not always the case… at least that's how it works for me. The reality is that some of us are insecure in our roles as leaders, and we are fearful of the young, up-and-coming leaders. We shouldn't be though, if we use the old business axiom of trying to hire someone better than ourselves. If they rise above you, celebrate their success. Want the best for them.

I wish I could say I always wanted the best for others, but that isn't the case. I regret that. But I have grown over the years. One good example is with Chris, I have always wanted the best for him.

I hired him right out of college, and he had the God-given DNA of an outstanding leader. He had the charisma, the willingness to take risks, and the humility to listen to others. These, along with many other qualities, made Chris a great leader. I thought Chris would replace me one day as the Maryland State Director, but he was chosen to be the Pennsylvania State Director and then a few years later, the Mid-Atlantic Vice President. Today, he is the youngest field Vice President out of fourteen leaders, making him my boss. He is truly a great boss, and I love working for him.

APPROACHABLE VERSUS UNAPPROACHABLE

When I think about the people I enjoy being with, I think about humble people. They are approachable. It doesn't matter that they have a higher position in the organization. It doesn't matter that they make millions more than I do. It doesn't matter that they own multiple homes. It doesn't matter if their kids go to private school. Because they have a humble heart, they are approachable. They value others and make time for me. Are you humble? Maybe another question to determine your humility is, are you approachable?

I think of Brent Price, a former NBA player that was making millions, yet, he drove a Toyota Camry. When he played for the Washington Bullets (now called the Wizards), he began to attend a church where I was serving and we got to know each other. When we were deciding where to go to lunch one day, he suggested we go to a certain restaurant because he had a coupon. What NBA player uses coupons? A humble one. And a frugal one. Humble people act just like everyday folks.

I think of billionaire and Walmart founder, Sam Walton, who drove an old pick-up truck with no air conditioning and lived in a humble home that some say anyone with a job could afford. He probably did it to make himself "normal," which made him approachable. I heard a story about him during his later years as CEO, when he visited a store and saw messy shelves. He got some employees together, sat on the floor to get everyone at the same level, and discussed the importance of the presentation on the shelves. That is a sign of humility.

Humility is such an interesting thing in life, and especially in the workplace where we spend a lot of time and work toward gaining confidence and knowledge. Yet, to truly apply the Coach Approach, we need to demonstrate genuine humility to everyone around us. The result will be growth in them, growth in us, and ultimately, growth in our organizations.

WISDOM FROM OTHERS

"Humility, I have learned, must never be confused with meekness. Humility is being open to the ideas of others."

– Simon Sinek –

"The X-Factor of great leadership is not personality; it's humility."

– Jim Collins –

"It takes humility to realize that we don't know everything, not to rest on our laurels and know that we must keep learning and observing."

– Cher Wang, CEO CTC –

WISDOM FROM THE WORD

"Do nothing out of selfish ambition or conceit, but in humility consider others as more important than yourselves. Everyone should look not to his own interests, but rather to the interests of others."

– Phil. 2:3-4 (CSB) –

"Therefore I, the prisoner in the Lord, urge you to walk worthy of the calling you have received, with all humility and gentleness, with patience, bearing with one another in love, making every effort to keep the unity of the Spirit through the bond of peace."

– Ephesians 4:1-3 (CSB) –

"For by the grace given to me, I tell everyone among you not to think of himself more highly than he should think. Instead, think sensibly, as God has distributed a measure of faith to each one."

– Romans 12:3 (CSB) –

TIME FOR ACTION

Reflect on times you have demonstrated humility.

_____

_____

_____

Reflect on the things you need to change to demonstrate
more humility.

_____

_____

_____

What is a powerful question you want to ask yourself as a leader
regarding humility?

_____

_____

_____

Based on what you learned in this chapter, complete this
sentence:

I will _____

_____

CHAPTER 8

EMPATHY / SELFLESSNESS

Empathy is the ability to understand and share the feelings of another.

It has been said that people don't care how much you know until they know how much you care. This is also true in leading. There is a component of leading that requires us to listen well and reflect back to the talent that we hear their pain. As we listen intently, we may need to reply with an empathetic statement versus a question. For example, "It sounds as if you are super frustrated with your supervisor, or it sounds as if this has made you really mad."

What does being empathetic do? It lets others know you are listening. It causes them to open up, and therefore, share more deeply with you. And deeper sharing can often lead to better answers to those important questions. It also builds trust. And trust is huge in the leader-talent relationship. A word of caution, though, if this leads down a road of bringing up deep past hurts related to this current person or issue, it may be time for them to see a counselor.

During one of my coaching sessions, the talent was super frustrated with her current boss. She was frustrated because he was not empathetic nor relational; when we got a chance to connect and talk, I listened intently to her frustration. I repeated back to her some of her frustrations I heard her say, and she replied to me that I got it. That set the whole coaching conversation up for success, because she realized I understood her; I was empathetic. From there it didn't matter what the topic was, there was a trust built out of empathy. **And empathy is a foundational posture that all leaders must have to be successful in the Coach Approach.**

STAND IN THEIR SHOES

> "EMPATHY IS ABOUT STANDING IN SOMEONE ELSE'S SHOES, FEELING WITH HIS OR HER HEART, SEEING WITH HIS OR HER EYES. NOT ONLY IS EMPATHY HARD TO OUTSOURCE AND AUTOMATE, BUT IT MAKES THE WORLD A BETTER PLACE."
>
> – DANIEL H. PINK –

Recently I was at the gym, and I saw one of my friends whom I've been trying to connect with for awhile. I asked him what he was doing that afternoon so we could grab coffee, but he said he could not get together because he was going to a funeral. I quickly moved on to suggest other times to meet. Then I began to think about this chapter on empathy, and I realized I showed zero empathy toward what he had just told me. He was going to a funeral, and I blew right by the statement onto the next thing. Someone with empathy would have paused and said, "Funeral? Who died? What happened? Are you going to be okay?"

I have lots of growing to do. How about you?

When we demonstrate empathy, we stand in their shoes. It's so crucial to the Coach Approach to understand what people are going through at the moment you are engaged in a conversation.

IT'S NOT ABOUT YOU

Being selfless is when your heart posture is more concerned about someone else's well-being and wishes than your own. This is critical from a leadership standpoint. Coaching is about your people, not about you. It is about their agenda and what they are bringing to you. As a supervisor, you are naturally going to want to tell them which direction to go in and which solution to pursue, but you need to refrain from that. What you can do is take the Coach Approach to ask some clarifying questions. Empathy will make coaching about them, and not about you.

DEEPEN THE CONNECTION

When we are empathic, we develop a deeper connection with our talent, which will lead to more conversations because empathy shows we get it. Empathy tells our talent we truly understand their problems and struggles. Empathy shows you are not some boss up in the ivory tower of leadership who is calling the shots and totally out of touch with the real world on the front lines of the organization. Talent who feel they are understood and cared for are more likely to give you their all and then some. Additionally, people will be more likely to stay with your organization if they feel heard and understood.

Recently, I was talking to a sports coach who was struggling with the lack of empathy from his leader. He was working 90-hour weeks, including Christmas morning, for the team's success, yet the leader did not share an ounce of empathy toward the frustration of missing so much family time and major family events. This demotivated the coach and his desire to excel. Other programs who offered sports coaching at the same level were more attentive to their coaches' needs and allowed their coaches to step away from a meeting or practice to be at their children's school events. They also realized the downside of taking away family time on holidays. The difference in leadership made all the difference in the two organizations.

What are you doing as a leader that is not demonstrating empathy to your staff, and therefore potentially demotivating them?

CURIOSITY CAN EXPAND OUR EMPATHY

I believe curiosity always moves us out of our comfort zones. When we go outside of our comfort zones, we grow, we learn new things, and we become more empathetic.

Practice growing your empathy through curiosity by talking to a stranger or someone with a different worldview from your own. Recently, I have been challenged to step outside my comfort zone and introduce myself to strangers. Last week, I was at a fast food restaurant and saw someone sitting by themselves with several duffle bags. I was prompted to go over and introduce myself. "How are you doing?" I asked. He replied, "I'm doing fine." I followed up by asking him, "How are you really doing?" The man told me about his struggles with drugs and that he was fresh out of a month in rehab. He and a friend both overdosed while using Fentanyl, and his friend did not recover. "I've let my two sons down. I'm waiting for my mom to pick me up to take me back home. Actually, I'm pretty stressed out right now."

My curiosity about this stranger led to a conversation I would have never imagined. The conversation honestly led to a new level of empathy for me since I had never met anybody in a situation like his. I asked if I could pray for him, and afterwards I gave him my number and told him I was just a phone call away for prayer or if he ever found himself in a situation where he was having trouble resisting the urge to do drugs.

Maybe you need to have a conversation with a stranger or someone unlike you to grow in the area of empathy.

REMOVE JUDGMENT

I have found it is incredibly hard to be empathetic if I am judgmental. Judging puts us in a place where it is almost impossible to listen well, understand, and be empathic. Take the example of the employee who always seems tired, and therefore, is performing at a lower level than you think they should. As a judger, I go down a road of building a narrative that may not be true at all. He is lazy. He is undisciplined and not getting a good night's sleep. He may be staying up drinking too much. We build this totally wrong narrative.

Then we have a conversation about their performance to get them to come in on time, be attentive in meetings, and stop yawning all day. But there is something deeper. We might even ask the question, "What is the deeper issue here?" "What is going on in your life that is causing this?" Then you find out he is driving an hour away every night after work to care for an aging parent. Or he has had to step in and help more with his kids because his wife started a second job to get rid of their debt.

We need to focus on listening with care, concern, and understanding, not only because it is the right thing to do, but it is a better way to lead your team. Your empathy will lead your team to give more of who they are to the organization. Empathy is something that takes a lifetime to master, but the important thing is getting on the road to get better.

STARVE THE JUDGER

How can we starve the judger inside of us? First, start with self-reflection of who we are, what we believe, and how we grew up. We probably need to reflect on previous generations of our family that have shaped our worldview. Second, we need to have self-awareness that we have biases that will lead to judgment more than empathy. Finally, approach conversations with a readiness to demonstrate grace. A simple way to look at grace is unmerited favor. Maybe the talent we are working with doesn't necessarily deserve what we are about to do for them, but in an effort to starve the judger, we demonstrate grace. This is not an exhaustive list, but it's a good start.

What do you need to do to starve the judger inside of you?

WISDOM FROM OTHERS

"I've learned that people will forget what you said, people will forget what you did, but people will never forget how you made them feel."

– Maya Angelou –

"Leadership is about empathy. It is about having the ability to relate to and connect with people for the purpose of inspiring and empowering their lives."

– Oprah Winfrey –

"Could a greater miracle take place than for us to look through each other's eyes for an instant?"

– Henry David Thoreau –

WISDOM FROM THE WORD

"and walk in the way of love, just as Christ loved us and gave himself up for us as a fragrant offering and sacrifice to God."

– Ephesians 5:2 (NIV) –

"And let us consider one another to provoke unto love and to good works: Not forsaking the assembling of ourselves together, as the manner of some is; but exhorting one another: and so much the more, as ye see the day approaching."

– Hebrews 10:24-25 (KJV) –

"Be happy with those who are happy, and weep with those who weep."

– Romans 12:15 (NLT) –

TIME FOR ACTION

Reflect on ways you are demonstrating empathy well.

_____

_____

_____

Reflect on the things you need to change to demonstrate
more empathy.

_____

_____

_____

What is a powerful question you want to ask yourself as a leader
regarding empathy?

_____

_____

_____

Based on what you learned in this chapter, complete this
sentence:

I will _____

_____

CHAPTER 9

SELF-CONTROL / PATIENCE

> "THE ABILITY TO CONTROL ONESELF, IN PARTICULAR ONE'S EMOTIONS AND DESIRES OR THE EXPRESSION OF THEM IN ONE'S BEHAVIOR, ESPECIALLY IN DIFFICULT SITUATIONS."
>
> – BY LEXICO.COM –

Self-control is a key characteristic of an effective coach, but it's one of the hardest to implement. Sally, a young staff member walks down the hall to ask you a question. You are most likely not sitting there waiting for questions, you are focused on your work. When the question or questions come from Sally, how are you feeling? Maybe annoyed at the interruption, maybe anxious because you have a deadline, or maybe frustrated thinking, *I can't believe she came down here again.*

With that mindset, what do you want to do? Get rid of Sally as fast as possible by blurting out the answers. But you missed the opportunity for her to self-discover the answer, because you lacked self-control and patience.

What are your options?

1. Give Sally the answers and move on. You missed the opportunity to coach her to the best possible solution.
2. Take the time and coach her up right then and there.
3. Realize this is going to take more time than you have and ask her if this can wait until you both have time to address this in the best way.

Self-control would lead you to ask Sally a few questions so you can offer her the best response. You could ask her a clarifying question if you want to answer her right away: "Sally, so what you are asking me is__?" To delay the conversation because you want to take the Coach Approach, you could say, "Sally, can this wait until__?"

Self-control will be one of the most challenging heart postures for us to live out because our nature is to tell others the answer and move on. But coaching requires us to pause, think, listen intently, be curious, and ask powerful questions. If you believe this is the better way, then you will need self-control to live it out.

SILENCE IS GOLD

I've seen the incredible power of silence during coaching. You and I probably don't think of silence as powerful, but it is. The only way you and I will get to the point of embracing silence is if we have self-control. Human nature, for me, wants to fill the gaps of silence. So many of us feel uncomfortable with silence, yet there's power in it to discover.

Let's think about this. If you can take the time to allow for silence, what happens to you as the person who is coaching? One thing that happens is it will enable you to think without having to listen. Often we're thinking about the next question to ask, therefore, not listening actively. The pause in the conversation allows you to think about a possible next question and, even in your mind, evaluate how this conversation is going or read into what is not being said by the talent, perhaps revealing the deeper issue.

From a talent standpoint, silence could mean I don't understand the question you asked. If that's the case, be patient; let them step in and say I don't understand the question. But if they don't say that, they're probably thinking about their situation and response, which is a good thing. That's right where you want to be.

Silence is uncomfortable, but silence can be powerful. On occasion, I have seen a person so uncomfortable with silence they just start filling in the silence with words. Words that don't necessarily make sense. Words that don't necessarily add value to the conversation. At this point, I need to explain to them the power of silence and let them know it might feel awkward that they're staring at me and I'm staring at them; **but in the silence, our brains are working, and our hearts are connecting to something deeper inside us.** Now we're getting into some awesome coaching. So let them know that you're aware of the discomfort, but you want them to relax in it. It has been quoted many times, *silence is an opportunity to become comfortable with the uncomfortable.*

SILENCE TAKES EVERYONE DEEPER

Just the other day, there were several times during my coaching sessions that I had the self-control (I don't always have it) to be silent, still, and wait for the talent to respond. The 5-7 seconds felt like minutes. That's ok. Something powerful was happening. The talent was thinking. This is one of the wonderful things that happens in a coaching session. You create moments to stop and think. It started with a question. "Is there a deeper issue?" This question can be powerful if we wait in silence, attentive for their answer.

TIME TO BE PATIENT

Patience can be defined as the ability to accept or tolerate delays, problems, or suffering without becoming annoyed or anxious.

Another important quality of a leader taking the Coach Approach is to be patient, which is hard because many people in leadership roles are not patient. They are hard-charging, Type-A people who get things done quickly, and being patient is not in their DNA. Why is this important? Because out of patience and taking your time, some of the best ideas come at the last second.

By exercising patience, I have had some of my best results from coaching conversations. What do I mean? As I am in the coaching conversation, often I am not sure where the conversation is going to go. Or how it is going to end. If I am patient, often near the end of the conversation, we will hit that "Ah ha" moment when the talent says, "Yes, that is what I need to do." This new awareness would not come about if I hadn't been patient.

BUILD THAT MUSCLE

Self-control is like a muscle. The more you work at it, the stronger it gets. I just started back at the gym to lift weights for the first time in many years. It feels great. The more I go, the stronger I get. Of course, that is no surprise. I think self-control is a little like lifting weights—the more times I get in a conversation and control my desire to talk and focus on listening, the more natural it becomes to be a listener versus a talker. The more times I follow up with a question versus interjecting my opinions, the more it becomes second nature to me. I challenge you to refrain from sharing about yourself and continue asking questions when you are in conversations over the next 24 hours. Practice your self-control.

WISDOM FROM OTHERS

"God's supernatural self-control is available
to us when we walk by the Spirit."

– Elizabeth George –

"Self control is the exercise of inner strength under
the direction of sound judgment that enables us to do,
think and say the things that are pleasing to God."

– Jerry Bridges –

"God has equipped you to handle difficult things. In
fact, He has already planted the seeds of discipline
and self-control inside of you. You just have to water
those seeds with His word to make them grow."

– Joyce Myers –

WISDOM FROM THE WORD

"for God gave us a spirit not of fear but of
power and love and self-control."

– 2 Timothy 1:7 (ESV) –

"A man without self-control is like a city
broken into and left without walls."

– Proverbs 25:28 (NIV) –

"But the fruit of the Spirit is love, joy, peace, patience,
kindness, goodness, faithfulness, gentleness, and
self-control. The law is not against such things."

– Galatians 5:22-23 (CSB) –

TIME FOR ACTION

Reflect on ways you are demonstrating self-control well.

_____

_____

_____

Reflect on the things you need to change to demonstrate more self-control.

_____

_____

_____

What is a powerful question you want to ask yourself as a leader regarding self-control?

_____

_____

_____

Based on what you learned in this chapter, complete this sentence:

I will _____

_____

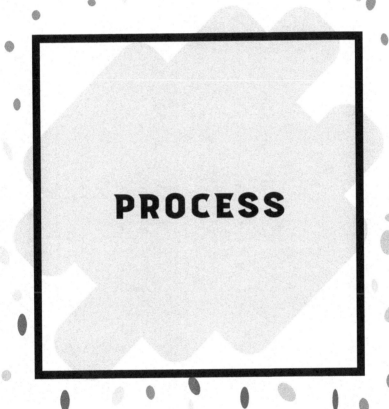

PROCESS

PART 3

PROCESS

You've reached the phase of the Coach Approach where things start to get exciting! Possibilities expand our vision about what could happen, leading us to have a growth mindset, think differently, and believe in the talent. A heart and mind posture that is quick to listen and ask questions will set you up for success. Now, it's time to put this all into action.

When you're actually leading somebody, what is that going to look like? In many ways, it looks like a simple conversation. Creating awareness during a conversation, and identifying action steps that need to be taken based on the conversation, is how to put the Coach Approach into process.

CHAPTER 10

OUTCOME

Outcome is about clarifying the win for your talent. It's important to focus on defining your talent's win, not your win. The conversations you'll engage in as part of the coaching process are not about you, they're about them. Sometimes I ask my talent this question: "What is the result you want from our conversation?" Another good question is: "What outcome do you want from our conversation?" These questions, and some similar aims, get us heading in the right direction.

The amount of time you have for the conversation will determine the amount of time you spend clarifying the result or outcome of the conversation. For example, if you have three minutes in an impromptu conversation in the hallway, you'll spend 30 to 60 seconds determining the outcome. If someone schedules a 30-minute meeting with you in your office, you might spend 5 to 10 minutes determining the outcome.

Please note that it's not uncommon for the first thing the talent to lay out as their win or outcome to be is inaccurate. Why do I say this? Often there's a deeper or more important issue that needs to be focused on first before addressing the topic they bring up. Therefore, take a few minutes to ask some questions from different angles to get them to wrestle deeply with the outcome they want and make sure it lines up with what they really need.

DON'T RUSH

Determining the outcome in advance is so important because it's the starting point for the Coach Approach. You won't know what end result to shoot for if you skip this step. Kicking off a conversation by defining outcomes will give you time to implement patience and self-control. Leaders often want to rush through this part of the Coach Approach. This is not a good idea. Rushing won't allow you to have a good start to the conversation, and it will often lead to poor endings. We need to have clarity on the outcome. When we have clarity on the outcome, when we're done with a conversation, we will feel successful because we understand the outcome or results our talent desires.

INTENTIONAL CONVERSATION

How many times have you had a conversation with someone on your staff and you felt as if you just went around in circles and didn't get anywhere? Would discussing an outcome or a result have made a difference in the conversation?

My coaching mentor, Keith Webb, in his book "The COACH Model" shares some key advice regarding outcomes. "A clear destination, or outcome, is one of the distinguishing features of coaching and one that makes the conversation intentional."

Let's unpack Keith's definition. The word "clear" is important. Having a clear outcome stated by the talent empowers you as the leader to move forward with gusto as you create awareness. The second important word is "intentional." Clear outcomes allow for intentional focus during the conversation, and this sets you up to lead toward a successful ending with clear action steps.

I would be embarrassed to share how many conversations I have had over the years with staff—both before I knew the Coach Approach and a few after —where we didn't clarify the outcome of our conversation. Therefore, our conversation was all over the map. At the end of these discussions, I felt like we didn't accomplish anything, and we were going around and around in circles.

FROM TIMID TO CONFIDENT

JoJo was given the opportunity to share his vision and results of his work in the Philippines to 60 people from around the world via Zoom. This was an exciting opportunity for him. JoJo is a former basketball coach at many levels, so I told him to just pretend this was a half-time locker room talk. I thought that would put him at ease, and he would give a very inspirational message. To my surprise, JoJo had too many slides and stories in his presentation; and worst of all, he read the whole presentation. The next day we got on the phone to debrief. He knew he didn't do well, and he humbly confessed he had fallen short. I began to take the Coach Approach: listen, be curious, and ask powerful questions.

Years ago, I would have taken the tellers approach. I would have told him all the things to fix and felt really good about the help I offered. But that would not have been the best way to help him. He would have left our meeting feeling defeated and embarrassed, and it's unlikely he would volunteer to present again. The better way was to take the Coach Approach, which brought encouragement, made him feel heard, and asked questions so he felt able to address his weaknesses and see the possibilities.

He was afraid of not achieving perfection; but in reality, any information he gave or stories he shared would have been 'perfect' because the audience had not previously heard his stories.

I wanted to go deeper with JoJo. "What is really important as far as your delivery of this message?" As he thought about it, he said his nonverbal communication. I said, "Tell me more," (a great follow-up question to get people to go deeper with their thinking). He thought about it for a minute before answering. "My voice inflection, leaning in with my body, using my hands and my face to communicate the message. Those are more important than the words I say." JoJo hit the nail on the head. He knew the answers, but as a coach, I needed to draw them out of him with questions. If over 80% of all communication is nonverbal, then anyone delivering a message must be concerned with their nonverbal communication just as much as their verbal message.

As we discussed more, I challenged him to give a small part of the message to just his staff so he could practice again and model for them the right way to do it versus the wrong way, which is what we saw before. He agreed and reported back to me several days later how great it felt to deliver the message in a more powerful way. After talking about how to make something simple for us to remember, we came up with this:

> ## PASSION & PERFORMANCE > PERFECTION

Think about how JoJo felt when he self-discovered a better way. Not only did that make him feel encouraged, but he owned the solution. All of that might have been missed if I had taken the teller approach; but through the Coach Approach, JoJo self-discovered the answers best for himself. Therefore, he was more than likely to implement his discoveries versus the one his supervisor told him. He felt empowered because they were his ideas.

EXPLORE AND CONFIRM

As we wrap up the conversation regarding the outcome, it is good to explore and confirm. A good exploration question is, "What would achieving this do for you?" This question will reveal the motivation or the "why" for the talent and the issue before them. The final step is to have them confirm the outcome by restating it to you. You could ask them, "Can you clarify for us the outcome you want from today's conversation?"

I cannot over-emphasize the importance of having a clear outcome decided by the talent. Starting off in the right direction will lead to a more successful conversation. This must be decided in the beginning of the conversation; and as the leader, you need to take on the responsibility of leading your talent.

WISDOM FROM OTHERS

"All Coaches have one thing in common, it's that they are ruthlessly results oriented."

– Fast Company Magazine –

"A great coach not only inspires but supports and encourages others to get results."

– Richard Schuy –

"The formulation of the problem is often more essential than its solution."

– Albert Einstein –

WISDOM FROM THE WORD

"When Jesus turned and noticed them following him, he asked them, 'What are you looking for?' They said to him, 'Rabbi' (which means 'Teacher'), 'where are you staying?' 'Come and you'll see,' he replied. So they went and saw where he was staying, and they stayed with him that day. It was about four in the afternoon."

– John 1:38-39 (CSB) –

"Jesus stopped, called them, and said, 'What do you want me to do for you?' 'Lord,' they said to him, 'open our eyes.' Moved with compassion, Jesus touched their eyes. Immediately they could see, and they followed him."

– Matthew 20:32-34 (CSB) –

"Then the mother of Zebedee's sons approached him with her sons. She knelt down to ask him for something. 'What do you want?' he asked her. 'Promise,' she said to him, 'that these two sons of mine may sit, one on your right and the other on your left, in your kingdom."

– Matthew 20:20-21 (CSB) –

TIME FOR ACTION

Reflect on ways you have helped others determine what they really want (outcome).

_____

_____

_____

Reflect on the things you need to change to improve at helping others determine their outcome.

_____

_____

_____

What is a powerful question you want to ask yourself as a leader regarding outcomes?

_____

_____

_____

Based on what you learned in this chapter, complete this sentence:

I will _____

_____

CHAPTER 11

AWARENESS

A significant part of awareness is asking powerful questions. Unfortunately, not all questions are powerful. Not all questions are equal. We can all grow in the area of asking great questions. We all ask questions every day, but good questions require us to pause and think about how to craft a thought-provoking question. First, to ask a powerful question, you have to know the clear outcome desired from the conversation. Second, you need to listen actively to know what question to ask next. Powerful questions will come when you know how to both lead and listen.

HOW DO YOU RATE YOUR LISTENING?

Awareness as a leader involves listening actively and recognizing what the talent is saying and not saying. Recently I was being coached; and as I answered my coach's questions, I began, without realizing it, to use some words repeatedly. Late into our conversation, my coach told me I had used the same word five times in ten minutes. She was actively listening to me, and because of that, she was able to redirect the focus in our conversation with her questions. The real issue was brought to the forefront by her skills of excellent listening and asking powerful questions.

ASKING POWERFUL QUESTIONS

I can tell you, as a coach, nothing makes me happier than when my talent says, "That was a powerful question." Because **powerful questions bring you to new heights of awareness,** prompt you to look at the issue from a different angle, and make you want to challenge the status quo. Even in regular conversations now, when I'm not coaching, I challenge myself to think of meaningful and impactful questions to ask as I'm listening during a conversation. Let's become great at asking questions, you can never practice too much.

ARE YOU A MEMBER OF TA?

Recently I got the opportunity to meet Bob. Bob was genuine, honest, and transparent in that he started our conversation by confessing that he was a part of TA. When he asked me if I also belonged to TA, I was a little embarrassed; but I had to admit I had no clue what that meant. He went on to tell me TA stood for Tellers Anonymous and that he had been a part of Tellers Anonymous for most of his life.

I am in recovery from being a lifelong teller. Ever since I realized I was a teller, I knew I had to make a change for the betterment of my relationships. That led me to think about how to lead with questions instead of cutting in to share and missing out on two-sided conversations. When I could tell that my family, friends, and coworkers saw the change in me and our communication blossomed, I said goodbye forever to being a teller.

What I've found in my life is, if you're a good teller, you rise up in the ranks in your organization, but you only create more tellers. New tellers don't create new and innovative ideas or move your organization forward with new possibilities. You don't help your team "think outside the box" when you lead by telling.

This is why I love the Coach Approach. If you are an influencer, CEO, VP, manager, or any other kind of leader, and you want different results, you're going to have to do things differently. It's time to ditch exclusively being a teller and lead with questions.

QUESTIONS DURING COVID-19

Like many others in 2020, I got COVID-19. In January 2020, COVID-19 came to the USA as a devastating virus. Late in March 2020, the World Health Organization declared this outbreak a pandemic. COVID-19 wiped me out for five days, I was unable to get out of bed or have a productive conversation. It just so happened that everyone in my family was gone during this time. Some friends knew that and asked if I needed anything or if they could drop something off. I replied to each well-meaning friend with a chorus of "I'm fine," not wanting anyone to go out of their way for me. Then my friend Sally called at 2:00pm to ask a question with the same intent, but she asked it differently. "Who is bringing dinner over tonight?" I replied no one is bringing dinner over. She said, "I am going to drop dinner off at 5:00pm." Over a year later, I remember this so vividly because her question was different from everyone else's. The same concept spoken differently prompted a different response and a different outcome. Be thoughtful in each question you ask.

ASK MORE QUESTIONS

I have heard it said that the average child asks 125 questions a day. The average adult asks 6. We need to tap into our childlike curiosity and ask more questions. Jesus, the leader of all leaders, asked 183 questions in the Gospels alone. He asked more questions than He answered. Often He answered questions with a question. There is so much wisdom in that. You and I have a habit of giving answers and telling, but we need to develop a new habit of being curious and asking questions. Leadership is not about telling people what to do, it's about developing leaders; and the way we develop leaders is to ask questions to get them to think through what could be the possible solutions.

SPIN HIM AROUND

After several coaching sessions with Grace, I asked her to describe coaching and this is what she said:

"Coaching for me was you spinning me around causing me to look at my situation from different angles. By your questions, you poked holes in what I was thinking. When I stopped spinning around, I saw my situation, my problem, and my issue in a different way. This allowed me to put together my own personal action steps to move forward and overcome the challenges I had shared in the beginning of the coaching."

WISDOM FROM OTHERS

"Coaching is unlocking a person's potential to maximize their own performance. It is helping them to learn rather than teaching them."

– Timothy Gallwey –

"Life begins at the end of your comfort zone."

–Neale Donald Walsh –

"Building awareness and responsibility is the essence of good coaching."

– John Whitmore –

WISDOM FROM THE WORD

"After three days, they found him in the temple sitting among the teachers, listening to them and asking them questions."

– Luke 6:46 (CSB) –

"And one of them, an expert in the law, asked a question to test him."

– Matthew 22:35 (CSB) –

"But wanting to justify himself, he asked Jesus, 'And who is my neighbor?'"

– Luke 10:29 (CSB) –

TIME FOR ACTION

Reflect on ways you are asking thoughtful and impactful questions.

_____

_____

_____

Reflect on the things you need to change to improve the questions you ask.

_____

_____

_____

What is a powerful question you want to ask yourself, as a leader, regarding asking better questions?

_____

_____

_____

Based on what you learned in this chapter, complete this sentence:

I will _____

_____

CHAPTER 12

ACTION STEPS

The final component of the Coach Approach process is action steps. The Coach Approach is about many things, but taking action based on the conversation is crucial. If you miss this part, you will have missed applying the results of the conversation.

Action steps will look different from conversation to conversation, but the important thing is that you and your talent know they can be accomplished. Some use the SMART goals to help them formulate their action steps. This acronym is very simple, but it will help you to know that your steps are realistic and can be completed.

Specific
Measurable
Achievable
Relevant
Time bound

4 SIMPLE TESTS

The very first book I read on coaching was *Leadership Coaching* by Tony Stoltzfus. In his book, he lays out 4 simple tests you can use to evaluate an action step:

"1. The **Clarity** test: I know exactly what I need to do.

2. The **Commitment** test: I will definitely do this.

3. The **Date Book** test: I have broken this down to where I can put it in my date book.

4. The **Deadline** test: I know when I've committed to have this done."

Let's say you just finished a conversation with a talent regarding hiring a new staff member to help him accomplish his goals for this year. Here are some action steps he may share at the end of your conversation:

1. *I will look into the steps to make a new hire.*

2. *I am going to process things by the end of the month.*

3. *Well, this whole hiring thing is interesting, probably going to be tough, but I guess I will try to call HR by Friday.*

4. *I will hire someone by the end of next month.*

5. *On Monday morning, I will turn in the job description to HR for posting.*

Let's look at these action steps that were submitted and evaluate them based on the 4 criteria: Clarity, Commitment, Date Book, and Deadline.

I will look into the steps to make a new hire.

The above action step fails the deadline criteria. Having no clear deadline will probably mean when you have your next conversation, nothing will have been done because they didn't choose a deadline.

I am going to process things by the end of the month.

The above action step fails the clarity test. If someone says they are going to "process things," that is about as vague as you can get. It is crucial that you have your talent bring as much clarity as possible to the action step. What is he going to process? How? By asking someone with experience? By researching on his own? Being specific will help you get more thorough results.

Well, this whole hiring thing is interesting, probably going to be tough, but I guess I will try to call HR by Friday.

The above action step fails the commitment criteria. Words like "probably" and "guess" are not words expressing a solid commitment to the action steps. I prefer them to use "I will" statements. "I will" statements are personal and demonstrate ownership and solid commitment.

I will hire someone by the end of next month.

This action step fails the date book criteria, which is about making sure your action step is so specific you could put it in your calendar. Therefore, this action needs to have a date attached to it.

On Monday morning, I will turn in the job description to HR for posting.

This action step fulfills all 4 criteria: Clarity, Commitment, Date Book, and Deadline. There is clarity in "turn in the job description." There is commitment in the "I will" statement. This fulfills the date book criteria because it is a focused simple step. Finally, there is a deadline of "Monday morning." This is an excellent example of a very well-crafted action step.

As a leader using the Coach Approach, you clarify an outcome, ask questions that create new awareness, and now, finish with some great action steps.

Action steps have to do with commitment and ownership. When your talent decides on their own action steps, they will have a higher likelihood of completing them. They will own it. Make sure to applaud them for creating these action steps, celebrate their commitment, and finally, hold them accountable to these action steps they designed. I have found when the talent embraces the Coach Approach, they become thankful for the accountability to help move things forward. There is much more commitment and ownership when the talent discovers the solution and formulates their own actions. This is another reason I believe the Coach Approach is the better way.

CLEAR ACCOUNTABILITY

Many times at work and following meetings, the action steps are not clear. Therefore, when we reconvene and discuss the results of the action steps people are confused because there was not clarity in the action steps. We must end each coaching conversation and each group meeting with clear action steps. This allows for accountability. For some the word accountability is a bad word, because they don't want accountability; or it has been applied to them unfairly in the past. I have experienced clear action steps that can lead to clear accountability. It is freeing because it doesn't feel good to be held accountable when I am not clear on my expectations. I think this concept should be applied to all leaders at the end of a group meeting. Many times we run out of time or just don't end the meetings with clear action steps. This means our talent goes back to their desk without clarity of what they must do and when it needs to be completed. We will move our teams forward with more unity, cooperation, and efficiency with clear accountability.

THINK INCREMENTAL

Action steps are also about change, and change is hard for many of us. While change can mean that our surroundings will not be the same, it often means that we will also have to think and act differently. Change also means progress and moving forward, and that is the goal of the Coach Approach. If the talent struggles with the action steps, maybe the change is too much. If this is the case, think about incremental change. Smaller steps can help the process seem a lot less daunting for someone with a big goal. As our talent creates these steps and we partner with them, you may ask the question: "In your heart are you going to be able to accomplish that step by that date?" If the answer is yes, celebrate and affirm them. If not, help them craft smaller action steps.

WISDOM FROM OTHERS

"The effectiveness of a leader is best judged
by the actions of those he guides."

– Bill Courtney –

"I absolutely believe that people, unless coached,
never reach their maximum capabilities."

– Bob Nardelli –

"A great coach not only inspires but supports
and encourages others to get results."

– Richard Schuy –

WISDOM FROM THE WORD

"So my people come to you in crowds, sit in front of you, and hear your words, but they don't obey them. Their mouths go on passionately, but their hearts pursue dishonest profit."

– Ezekiel 33:31 (CSB) –

"What good is it, my brothers and sisters, if someone claims to have faith but does not have works? Can such faith save him?"

– James 2:14 (CSB) –

"Do what you have learned and received and heard from me, and seen in me, and the God of peace will be with you."

– Philippians 4:9 (CSB) –

TIME FOR ACTION

Reflect on ways you are helping your talent get clear, tangible, date-driven action steps.

_____

_____

_____

Reflect on the things you need to change to improve your talent's action steps.

_____

_____

_____

What is a powerful question you want to ask yourself as a leader regarding creating better action steps?

_____

_____

_____

Based on what you learned in this chapter, complete this sentence:

I will _____

_____

PIVOT

PART 4

PIVOT

The final phase of the Coach Approach is implementing your new knowledge, leading you to pivot from your old style of leadership to this new style. This will have personal and corporate applications. There are new habits you need to focus on adding, and old habits that need to drop off.

CHAPTER 13

APPLICATION

PERSONAL APPLICATION

As you begin to pivot to a new approach, it's important to think through both personal applications and corporate applications. All of us, regardless of our jobs, are involved in the community, local organizations, and in our families. The Coach Approach can be applied to all areas of life.

WHAT COLLEGE SHOULD I GO TO?

As I was recently catching up with my friend, Andrew, I found out his daughter had begun the tough process of choosing a college. I remember clearly the challenges all four of my daughters tackled when it was time for them to do the same. We applied the Coach Approach principles at home, and it was beneficial. Let's take a look at how Andrew's daughter could apply the Coach Approach in a large personal decision such as choosing a college.

Outcome

Using our coaching structure, now is the ideal time to determine the outcome. She's not yet chosen a college, on-campus visits are going to start, and the timeline is set since she'll need to choose a college relatively soon.

From a big picture standpoint, *what outcome does she want?*
To find the right fit for college.

At a closer look, *what does she want from each on-campus visit?*
To see if the college is the one she wants to attend or not.

At an even closer look, *what outcome does she want from each meeting, event, and person she interacts with on campus?*
To see if this college fits the criteria she has created for her dream college.

So, an ideal outcome for her would look like this:

Awareness

After the outcome is established, addressing each aspect of the college decision process, there should be a significant amount of time spent asking questions from many angles to grow her awareness.

What are the best questions I need to ask others to determine if this college is the right fit for me? Has the college met the criteria I want?
Here are a few examples of some angle questions:

Family Angle: *How would choosing this college impact my relationships with my family?*

Financial Angle: *What would be the impact on me and my family financially if I choose this college?*

Future Angle: *How would attending this college impact my future? Job possibilities?*

Action Steps

Finally, after an outcome has been decided and new awareness has been discovered through answering many questions, she will need to take some specific action steps.

What are the things (calls, emails, research…) to do based on my visits to rank my top schools?

Here are a few sample action steps:

By this Friday morning, call the career center to learn about their process and results in helping graduates find a job.

By the end of the month, talk with 3–5 alumni to learn what they liked best about their experience as a student at this university.

By next month, go online to learn all the steps and the timeline from application to acceptance.

Choosing a college is one of many personal scenarios that benefit from applying the Coach Approach. Using the process—define the outcome, build awareness by asking questions, set action steps—will help her arrive at a confident and clear decision.

WHAT SHOULD MY NONPROFIT DO AT THIS DINNER?

Years ago, I took over a nonprofit, and I found out I was in charge of the annual fundraising dinner. The dinner had a lot of history, including many successes and failures. It was a huge event with many different facets, and I was now in charge of all of them. No pressure! To tackle the challenge, I applied the Coach Approach to the nonprofit dinner.

Outcome

What is the outcome we wanted from this dinner? Some said raising funds, new volunteers, awareness in the community, sharing the Gospel… that is too many outcomes. We needed to narrow our focus by asking more questions to determine the dinner's goal. We determined our defined outcome was to raise money.

Awareness

After we concluded that funding was our top priority, we began to ask questions to nail down the details. *What type of fundraising was it going to be? What type of people did we need to invite? Did we want to raise funds beforehand? Did we want to challenge with matching funds?*

Action Steps

After each planning meeting, we determined what action steps we needed to take and who would complete them. SMART goals were the perfect way to ensure everyone could accomplish their action step before the next meeting.

Here are a few examples:

By April 10th, we will determine the number of attendees for the event.

Before the next meeting, Matt will enlist 10 people to be on the welcome team.

By this Thursday, Lilly will email us the sponsors from the past 3 years.

Taking the Coach Approach led us to a very successful banquet that first year and many years to follow. I believe it was a success because we had a clearly defined outcome of raising a set amount of funds. Also, our whole team offered input and engaged in question-asking so we had a shared awareness about our fundraising focus. This allowed our team to feel valued and work together well. Finally, because we created clear action steps and followed through on them, we had an awesome team effort and even exceeded our goal.

I can share hundreds of scenarios where the Coach Approach offered a better way to lead at work, in life, and with teams. As you begin to take the Coach Approach, you may consider getting a mentor, coach, or another person to walk with you. It is always helpful to have someone challenge and encourage you when you are striving to implement something new in your life.

DEVELOP A COACHING CULTURE IN YOUR ORGANIZATION

More and more companies and nonprofits are adding coaching as a way to further develop their staff. Cru, Young Life, and Intervarsity are some of the ministries that have embraced coaching. Chick-Fil-A, Microsoft, and many other companies have adopted coaching as a critical way to help staff grow to the next level. Their desire is to have a coaching culture instead of a telling culture.

Culture is a buzzword in companies and sports teams. It is something easier seen than defined. I have read many definitions of culture, but the one I like the best is very simple: **Culture is language plus behavior.**

When I think of the sports team culture, I am reminded of the 2019 World Champions, the Washington Nationals. They used phrases like: "I believe we will win," "We got this," and "I love my teammates." What do I remember about their behavior? They were having fun, laughing, and taking the edge off those high-pressure moments. One of the things all Nationals fans loved was watching the team climbing into the dugout and acting like they were on a victory bus after a home run. Their language and behavior defined their culture.

What would it look like for your company or organization to have a coaching culture? As far as language and communication, there would be an increase in questions being asked, words of encouragement, and even some silence to allow the talent to reflect more. The behavior and thinking of staff would include a growth mindset, possibility thinking, listening actively, an empathic heart, and partnering to succeed. Culture is what you create or what you allow. You can create culture on purpose with intentionality or by accident without leadership.

WHAT ARE THE RESULTS?

Research released by the Association for Talent Development in 2014 revealed that coaching:

- Improves communication by 69%
- Raises engagement by 65%
- Enhances skills-to-performance by 63%
- Stimulates productivity by 61%
  - growth mindset to accomplish more and new things
  - clear action steps
  - accountability

What company doesn't want those things to happen inside their organization? In my experience, I've seen coaching have this impact on my talent. I've especially seen communication improve for many reasons.

1. Leaders begin to listen actively. Listening is such a critical role in leadership that we don't take seriously enough.
2. Communication improves when you allow for silence. Too many times, if there is more than one second of silence, we step in to fill the gap. Let the gap of silence

be. Thinking is happening, curiosity is building, and self-discovery is happening.

3. Your communication will improve because you are more aware of the distractions inhibiting you from having a good conversation.

The Coach Approach will raise the engagement of your employees because your culture will shift from focusing on telling to asking questions, allowing them to engage in the process of finding a solution. When we approach our staff with a heart of empathy, they know it. They feel it. Knowing that someone cares and is listening will amp up their engagement. Coaching will create an environment of allowing them to decide the next steps, which will help them create more ownership.

An additional benefit of adopting the Coach Approach will be enhancing the staff's skills to perform at a higher level. As you begin to look at each of your staff members, you will be able to determine the areas your team needs to grow and be challenged to change.

Taking this new approach will stimulate productivity. What are the possibilities and solutions to the obstacles in front of you? The implementation of creating clear action steps at the end of each coaching conversation alone will certainly boost productivity.

The Coach Approach is a partnership between the supervisor and his talent. This partnership leads to healthy conversations and healthy accountability.

This is a time to pause and truly consider the many ways the Coach Approach can be implemented into your personal life and with your organization. Narrow your ways down to one way, and focus on implementing that one concept. My philosophy is to start small but think big.

WISDOM FROM OTHERS

"Do one thing every day that scares you."

– Franklin Roosevelt –

"My powers are ordinary. Only my application brings me success."

– Sir Isaac Newton –

"When something is important enough, you do it even if the odds are not in your favor."

– Elon Musk –

WISDOM FROM THE WORD

"But someone will say, 'You have faith, and I have works. Show me your faith without works, and I will show you faith by my works."

– James 2:18 (CSB) –

"But be doers of the word and not hearers only, deceiving yourselves."

– James 1:22 (CSB) –

"Therefore, with your minds ready for action, be sober-minded and set your hope completely on the grace to be brought to you at the revelation of Jesus Christ."

– 1 Peter 1:13 (CSB) –

TIME FOR ACTION

Reflect on ways you have implemented coaching into your personal and work life.

_____

_____

_____

Reflect on the things you need to change to implement a new coaching concept into your personal and work life.

_____

_____

_____

What is a powerful question you want to ask yourself as a leader regarding implementing coaching into your personal and work life?

_____

_____

_____

Based on what you learned in this chapter, complete this sentence:

I will _____

_____

CHAPTER 14

HABITS

Over the years, I have become fascinated by the subject of habits. So much so that I have become a student of habits. As you think about pivoting to the Coach Approach, some habits you have must change. You may be freezing up or getting stressed right now, because you want to be that kind of leader that uses the principles laid out here, but you realize the Coach Approach isn't a habit yet. Or even worse, you may realize you have habits that seem easier to change, but you haven't been able to make progress in those habits yet. Relax, you can do this.

Before we start talking about new habits, we need to address changing how you see yourself. Most of you might not see yourself as a coaching leader yet, but I would like you to get there. It's important to know your new identity in order to implement the new habits you want. How are we going to accomplish this?

First is to write a mantra and read it every morning for 30 days. "I am a coaching leader." Maybe you want to create a list of mantras that you read each morning that will help shape the person you want to be.

Here are a few:

"I will love people and believe the best in them."

"I am disciplined."

"I will bring my best and then some."

"I will take care of my temple that the Lord has given me."

Second, every time you apply something from this book, say to yourself, "I am a coaching leader." It is going to help reinforce in your mind that you actually are a coaching leader, even if you are just beginning.

There is power in saying things out loud and there is overwhelming research and science to support that speaking out loud is a great way to rewire our brains. That's why to really see yourself as a coaching leader, you need to read the phrase, "I am a coaching leader" every morning. Your brain will embrace that and you will live more like a coaching leader.

THE BEST ADVICE I'VE EVER HEARD

I love the story my friend, Jon Gordon, shares in his book, *The Power of Positive Leadership*. Dr. James Gillis did something many would never ever think of doing—he competed in two Ironman triathlons back to back. You may think that is crazy, but he actually did this six times while in his fifties! When asked how he did it, he gave this advice: "I learned to talk to myself instead of listening to myself." You see, when we listen to ourselves, often the message is negative. In his case, he probably was hearing things like "you are too old" or "just quit, no one would blame you." But when he stopped listening to himself and started talking to himself with words of encouragement and positive phrases, he was able to complete the race.

What are the positive phrases you need to say to yourself to be the coaching leader you are called to be?

IT'S JUST LIKE RIDING A BIKE

Start with a beginner's mindset; be willing to fail and get back up and try again, just like in riding a bike. With any new skill, there will be failures. Set yourself a small daily coaching goal and try to stick to it for a week or two. You may surprise yourself!

A few examples to get you thinking:

1. The next time you find yourself listening to someone, use one of the questions I gave you: "Can you tell me more?" or "And what else?"

2. The next time someone comes to you with a problem, don't give the answer you know but ask them, "What do you think is possible?"

3. The next time you make a call from your desk or kitchen table, remove all objects, stacks of paper or work to be done out of sight so you can focus on the conversation.

THE POWER OF HABITS

I encourage anyone who wants to change a habit to read Charles Duhigg's fascinating book *The Power of Habits*. In the book, he talks about how at least 40% of what we do is a habit. We don't even think about most of what we do; our actions have become routine. He broke down habits into 3 stages: Cue, Routine, and Reward.

Cue: This is what triggers you to do the habit.
Routine: This is the behavior you automatically engage in.
Reward: This is a result of doing the routine.

A simple example of this is every morning I walk downstairs and see my coffee cup sitting in my coffee machine (the cue), and that leads me to go over and start the coffee machine (the routine) for a cup of delicious and wonderful-smelling coffee (the reward). On the mornings I am running behind and don't make it to the kitchen to see the cue (coffee cup ready to be filled in the machine), I don't have a cup of coffee from home because I didn't see the cue.

To change a habit, you need to start with changing the cue. Here are some changes I have made that have started new habits for me. My doctor prescribed some vitamins and medication that needed to be taken every morning and night. I kept forgetting to get them out of the cabinet, and so many days went by without me taking them. I was missing a cue! Now my cue is a pill holder that sits on my sink next to a glass for water. The cue works— every morning and evening, I see my pill box and my water (cue) that leads me to take the pills (routine); and now I will have a healthier life (reward).

WHAT COACHING HABITS DO YOU NEED TO START?

We could break down every section of this book and every component of coaching to evaluate what new habits you need to create, but we don't have the space to do that. Let's choose a few areas of focus.

Scenario #1: A staff person comes to you with a question about their priorities and what they should be focusing on next month.

Cue: A staff person asking you a question and you know the answer.

The old you responds:

Routine: Tell them what to do. The downside is they don't spend any energy or time wrestling with what they should be focusing on, they miss a growth opportunity and an opportunity to self-discover what needs to be done.

Reward: You feel great because your staff came to you with a question and you had the answer. You even feel great about your answer, therefore, you can't wait for the next time they come to you with a question.

The new you as a coaching leader responds:

Routine: You are curious and listen actively. Pause after you hear the question (cue). The new you is not going to give the answer right away, but is going to ask a question.

Reward: You feel great because you are learning a new habit, but more importantly you are helping your talent self-discover what they need to focus on. And because they are self-discovering, they are more likely to accomplish it.

Scenario #2: You ask an underperforming staff member to come and meet with you to figure out why they are performing poorly.

Cue: A poorly performing staff member is coming to my office, but I pretty much know what is going on already.

The old you:

Routine: I make assumptions of what I think the issue is. I am annoyed and uncaring. I ask a question or two.

Reward: I did what I needed to do to cover my back if my boss asks me about the situation.

The new you as a coaching leader responds:

Routine: I listen with empathy as I hear what is going on. I show more concern for my talent than I do for the results. I ask questions like, "What is the deeper issue here?"

Reward: I feel great because I truly cared about my talent more than the results, and they can tell. They feel better about our relationship because we got to the issue with some powerful questions from different angles, enabling us to move forward.

YOUR POTENTIAL

The potential of your leadership is a direct reflection of your daily habits. Now is a good time to look at some habits you want to change to help you become the best coaching leader you can be. Habits can be a superpower to take you places you haven't been before. We get what we repeat; and therefore, we need to look at what we are repeating. The potential for you to grow as a leader, help your people grow, and change the culture of your team is limitless. Based on personal experience, I know that if you focus on one habit at a time in the short term, the long term results will skyrocket.

WISDOM FROM OTHERS

"If I cannot do great things, I can do
small things in a great way."

– Rev. Dr. Martin Luther King, Jr. –

"The chains of habit are too light to be felt
until they are too heavy to be broken."

– Warren Buffett –

"Every action you take is a vote for the type
of person you wish to become."

– James Clear –

WISDOM FROM THE WORD

"Look, I am about to do something new; even now it is coming. Do you not see it? Indeed, I will make a way in the wilderness, rivers in the desert."

– Isaiah 43:19 (CSB) –

"For this reason, we must pay attention all the more to what we have heard, so that we will not drift away."

– Hebrews 2:1 (CSB) –

"Therefore, if anyone is in Christ, he is a new creation; the old has passed away, and see, the new has come!"

– 2 Corinthians 5:17 (CSB) –

TIME FOR ACTION

Reflect on your current coaching leader habits and the ones you are doing well.

_____

_____

_____

Reflect on the habits you need to change to be a better coaching leader.

_____

_____

_____

What is a powerful question you want to ask yourself as a coaching leader regarding your coaching habits?

_____

_____

_____

Based on what you learned in this chapter, complete this sentence:

I will _____

_____

CHAPTER 15

MISTAKES PEOPLE MAKE

As you step into the Coach Approach, your mind will be filled with all the dos and don'ts of coaching. Don't let yourself get overwhelmed by trying to implement everything at once. Just be yourself and try to incorporate one aspect of what you have learned each week, adding to your progress along the way. As with any new endeavor, mistakes will be made. The important thing is to learn from them by evaluating how we got to the point of making a mistake.

Some common mistakes I've seen:

1. **Too much talking, not enough listening.**
   You may naturally be a talker and advice-giver. That is not coaching. We should do 20% of the talking and 80% of the listening. Remember this is about the talent, and not us.

2. **Not allowing space for silence.**
   You are going to ask some amazing, thought-provoking questions that will make your talent stop and think. Let

there be space for silence. Don't interrupt or rescue them from the uncomfortable moment.

3. **Rushing through the outcome.**

   With the wrong outcome, the action steps will not be as impactful and have the potential to leave your true problem unsolved. The outcome should be determined before the conversation.

4. **Ending without action steps.**

   If the talent doesn't make a commitment to some date-defined action steps after the conversation, then we have missed a huge value of the conversation.

5. **Focusing on the technique of coaching versus the mindset.**

   90% of athletes' performance is driven by the mind. The same thing applies to leadership coaching. What is your mind telling you that impacts your coaching more than your technique of coaching?

6. **Forgetting to remove as many distractions as possible.**

   Remove distractions to be fully present, whether that is in your workplace or at home.

> YOU ARE GOING TO MAKE MISTAKES, BUT DON'T LET THEM DETER YOU. YOUR AIM IS NOT PERFECTION, YOUR AIM IS PROGRESS.

WISDOM FROM OTHERS

"No one became a great coach overnight. It takes years of consistent, intentional practice, studying and learning from mistakes accumulated along the way."

– Myke Celis, M.A., PCC –

"The road to high-performance and win-win partnerships has plenty of falling rocks, potholes, and detours. However, if you are able to read the road signs, you can steer around many of these obstacles."

– Center for Management & Organization Effectiveness –

"No leader likes admitting they make mistakes, let alone making the mistake and this is often the best way to learn."

– Anne Taylor –

WISDOM FROM THE WORD

"Don't worry about anything, but in everything, through prayer and petition with thanksgiving, present your requests to God. And the peace of God, which surpasses all understanding, will guard your hearts and minds in Christ Jesus."

– Philippians 4:6-7 (CSB) –

"Humble yourselves, therefore, under the mighty hand of God, so that he may exalt you at the proper time, casting all your cares on him, because he cares about you."

– 1 Peter 5:6-7 (CSB) –

"The one who conceals his sins will not prosper, but whoever confesses and renounces them will find mercy. Happy is the one who is always reverent, but one who hardens his heart falls into trouble."

– Proverbs 28:13-14 (CSB) –

THE COACH APPROACH

TIME FOR ACTION

Reflect on ways you are making some of the mistakes listed and some that may not be listed.

_____

_____

_____

Reflect on the things you need to change to remove some of the mistakes.

_____

_____

_____

What is a powerful question you want to ask yourself as a leader regarding mistakes?

_____

_____

_____

Based on what you learned in this chapter, complete this sentence:

I will _____

_____

CHAPTER 16

PRO TOOLS AND TIPS

Over the years, I have picked up tools and tips I want to pass along to you. These will help you be more effective in taking the Coach Approach. Just like you use different tools around the house for different functions, the same can be said of coaching tools. The more you use them, the more you know when and how to use them effectively.

W. I. N.

The W.I.N. model is used to evaluate meetings, events, and most things that will happen in your organization. This is a simple yet very effective tool. If you lead with this feedback tool, others will take it and use it to evaluate their happenings too. Evaluating something doesn't have to be stressful or unfocused. W.I.N. stands for:

Well. What went WELL in the meeting, event, or discussion?
Improve. What do I need to IMPROVE?
Next time. What should I do differently NEXT TIME?

COACH MODEL

The COACH Model was created by Keith Webb from Creative Results Management. This is a tool to be used if you want to go much deeper in the coaching journey than I took you in this book. My goal was to introduce you to the Coach Approach in a very simple way. This model and the book about it will take you to a whole new level of coaching. Keith trained me in this model, and it is what I use in my coaching practice.

Connect: This is the time you catch up with your talent and see how they are doing. It can also be a time to follow up on the previous session to see if they completed the action steps.

Outcome: This is where you clarify the outcome or the results for your time together.

Awareness: This is a time of active listening and asking powerful questions to create new awareness and gain insights into their challenges.

Course of Action: These are action steps decided by the talent. They need to be clearly defined with a date for them to be completed by.

Highlights: This is a chance to reflect on the coaching conversation including any "ah ha" moments.

MIND MAPPING

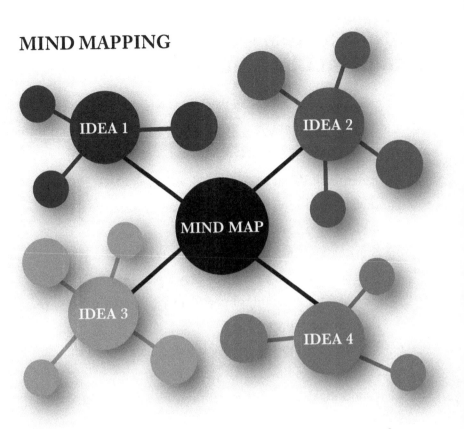

Mind mapping can be used for many things. I have used it as an individual and in group settings for brainstorming. I also used it to come up with the main themes for this book. I have used it in thinking through complex problems. I love using it to be creative and explore new ideas. The new ideas I have come up with when I am mind mapping a topic amazes me.

Mind mapping is an excellent tool to use with groups that are trying to solve a problem or determine what is possible. As your team works together, you will be surprised at the outcomes they discover because of everyone working together. Let the answers flow.

25 ANGLES FROM KEITH WEBB, CREATIVE RESULTS MANAGEMENT

Angles are different perspectives from which to discuss a situation. Any topic, category, or perspective could be formed into an Angle question. Here are 25 examples:

1. Relational: What are the relational dynamics?
2. Background: Step back for a moment, what are the underlying issues?
3. Spiritual: From a spiritual perspective, what do you see?
4. Culture: How might culture play a part in this situation?
5. Personality: How might personality (yours or others') be influencing things?
6. Financial: If money weren't an issue, how would that change things?
7. Emotion: What role do emotions play in this situation?
8. Intuition: What is your gut telling you?
9. Information: What additional information do you need?
10. People: Who might be able to give you a different perspective?
11. Organizational: How might your organizational structure be influencing things?
12. Environment: What things around you are holding you back?
13. Community: In what ways is your community impacting you?
14. Values: Which of your values are you trying to honor in this situation?

15. Calling: What parts of this connect to your calling?

16. Spouse: What does your spouse think about this?

17. Family: How is your family being affected in this situation?

18. Employer: Where does your boss fit in?

19. Experience: How have you handled this in the past?

20. Priority: How important is this to you?

21. Motivation: What would overcoming this situation do for you personally?

22. Loss: What do you have to give up to move forward?

23. Time: What difference would it make if you had 3 days/ months/ years?

24. Energy: Which parts of this give you energy?

25. Jesus: What would Jesus do?

TIME FOR ACTION

Reflect on ways you have used some of the models presented.

_____

_____

_____

Reflect on the ways you can use the models shared.

_____

_____

_____

What is a powerful question you want to ask yourself as a leader regarding implementing the W.I.N. Model, The COACH Model, or Mind Mapping?

_____

_____

_____

Based on what you learned in this chapter, complete this sentence:

I will _____

_____

END NOTES

CHAPTER 1

- Dweck, C. (2017). *Mindset - Updated Edition: Changing The Way You think To Fulfil Your Potential* (6th ed.). Little, Brown Book Group.
- Webb, K. E., & Collins, G. R. (2012). *The COACH Model for Christian Leaders: Powerful Leadership Skills to Solve Problems, Reach Goals, and Develop Others.* CreateSpace Independent Publishing Platform.

CHAPTER 3

- Mautz, S. (2021, January 5). *Google Tried to Prove Managers Don't Matter. Instead, It Discovered 10 Traits of the Very Best Ones.* Inc.Com. Retrieved July 22, 2022, from https://www.inc.com/scott-mautz/google-tried-to-prove-managers-dont-matter-instead-they-discovered-10-traits-of-very-best-ones.html

CHAPTER 4

- *The Link Between Curiosity and Success* – Kortivity. (n.d.). Kortivity. Retrieved July 22, 2022, from https://www.kortivity.com/blog/the-link-between-curiosity-and-success/

CHAPTER 5

- *The Gold Standard in Coaching | ICF - Core Competencies*. (2022, May 26). International Coaching Federation. Retrieved July 22, 2022, from https://coachingfederation.org/credentials-and-standards/core-competencies

- Stoker, J. (2013). *Overcoming Fake Talk: How to Hold REAL Conversations that Create Respect, Build Relationships, and Get Results* (1st ed.). McGraw Hill.

- Treasure, J. (n.d.). *Video 5 - RASA*. Julian Treasure. Retrieved July 22, 2022, from https://www.juliantreasure.com/5-part-video-series/rasa

CHAPTER 6

- Stanier, M. B. (2020, March 13). *How to tame your Advice Monster*. TED Talks. Retrieved July 22, 2022, from https://www.ted.com/talks/michael_bungay_stanier_how_to_tame_your_advice_monster?language=en

- Stanford University. (2014, April 24). *Stanford study finds walking improves creativity*. Stanford News. Retrieved July 22, 2022, from https://news.stanford.edu/2014/04/24/walking-vs-sitting-042414/

CHAPTER 7

- Blanchard, K., & Hodges, P. (2016). *Lead Like Jesus Revisited: Lessons from the Greatest Leadership Role Model of All Time* (Revised ed.). Thomas Nelson.

- Kern, K. (2017, December). *The Markers of a Humble Leader*. The Table Group. Retrieved July 22, 2022, from https://www.tablegroup.com/the-markers-of-a-humble-leader/

- Lencioni, P. (2017, December). *Serving up Humble, Hungry, Smart*. The Table Group. Retrieved July 22, 2022, from https://www.tablegroup.com/serving-up-humble-hungry-smart/

CHAPTER 9

- Oxford University Press (OUP). (n.d.). *Self-Control*. Lexico.Com. Retrieved July 22, 2022, from https://www.lexico.com/en/definition/self-control

CHAPTER 10

- Webb, K. E. (2012). *The COACH Model for Christian Leaders: Powerful Leadership Skills to Solve Problems, Reach Goals, and Develop Others*. Active Results LLC.

CHAPTER 12

- Stoltzfus, T. (2012, January 30). *An Effective Action Step: Four Tests*. Coach22. Retrieved July 22, 2022, from https://www.coach22.com/blogs/blog/an-effective-action-step-four-tests

CHAPTER 13

- Cole, M. (2020, November 18). *The Case for Developing Communication Skills in Managers: More Engagement, More Profits*. Association for Talent Development. Retrieved July 22, 2022, from https://www.td.org/insights/the-case-for-developing-communication-skills-in-managers-more-engagement-more-profits

CHAPTER 14

- Duhigg, C. (2017, November 20). *How Habits Work*. Charles Duhigg. Retrieved July 22, 2022, from https://charlesduhigg.com/how-habits-work/
- Gordon, J. (n.d.). *The Best Advice I've Ever Heard*. Jon Gordon's Weekly Newsletter. Retrieved July 22, 2022, from https://jongordon.com/positive-tip-best-advice.html

CHAPTER 16

- Webb, K. E. (2021, November 5). *50 Powerful Coaching Questions*. Keith Webb. Retrieved July 22, 2022, from https://keithwebb.com/50-powerful-coaching-questions/

- Webb, K. E. (2021, March 22). *The COACH Model®*. Keith Webb. Retrieved July 22, 2022, from https://keithwebb.com/coach-model/

- Webb, K. E. (2017, January 7). *Don't Give Feedback, Generate Feedback*. Keith Webb. Retrieved July 22, 2022, from https://keithwebb.com/how-to-give-feedback-by-generating-feedback/

ACKNOWLEDGMENTS

From day one, this project has been a team effort. I would first like to thank my wonderful wife **Rhonda** for being my number one cheerleader. She has been a tremendous sounding board and editor too. My girls, (**Sally, Grace, Lucy** and **Lilly**) you have captured my heart and my love. I am grateful for your constant encouragement to me in all of my endeavors. My friend of over thirty years, **Dan Britton,** thank you for challenging me, pushing me and giving me opportunities to write, train and speak. Your feedback continues to move me forward. **Jessica,** my author mentor and writing mentor from Two Penny Publishing, we did it. I can't believe it. I am grateful for your help every step of the way. To **Dick Savidge,** the first coach I ever hired. You told me: "You should become a coach." I am forever grateful you said that because it changed my life. **Tina Stoltzfus Horst** thank you for being my coach while I was writing this book and embodying all of the positive attributes of coaching shared in this book and many that are not shared here. **Tim Mellott** and **Pauley Hynes,** thanks for being brothers in Christ and iron sharpening iron for me. **Keith Webb** and **Charles "Beast Mode Coach" Hooper Jr.,** you guys are my teachers, coaching mentors and the ones I still look to to be challenged.

Well, I am sure I left some folks out but not intentionally. Finally, I am forever grateful for my **Heavenly Father** that has given me eternal life and guides me every day.

ABOUT THE AUTHOR

Coach Mark Stephens is a leader that develops leaders around the world through coaching, training, and speaking. As an ICF (International Coach Federation) ACC certified coach, he has a passion to serve others. He has coached sports (mostly wrestling and girls lacrosse) for over 35 years. He has been with Fellowship of Christian Athletes (FCA) since 1982 as volunteer and in many different staff roles including Maryland State Director and Mid-Atlantic International Director. He has been married over 31 years to his Honey, Rhonda. They have four daughters, two sons-in-law and one grandson.

He can be reached at www.coachmarkstephens.com